Touch

Touch

Tiffany Field

A Bradford Book
The MIT Press
Cambridge, Massachusetts
London, England

First MIT Press paperback edition, 2003

This book was set in Sabon by Best-set Typesetter Ltd., Hong Kong.

Printed and bound in the United States of America.

Library of Congress Cataloging-in-Publication Data

Field, Tiffany.
　　Touch / Tiffany Field.
　　　　p.　cm.
　　"A Bradford book."
　　Includes bibliographical references and index.
　　ISBN 978-0-262-06216-9 (hc. : alk. paper)—
978-0-262-56156-3 (pb. : alk. paper)
　　1. Touch—Psychological aspects.　2. Touch—Therapeutic use.　3. Massage therapy.　I. Title.
　　BF275 .F54 2001
　　152.1′82—dc21

　　　　　　　　　　　　　　　　　　　　00-068722

10　9　8　7　6

Contents

Preface

Someone once said that research is me-search, that we study problems that have personal meaning. This is true in my case. I first became interested in the problem of premature infants many years ago when my daughter was born prematurely. I continued in this interest later, when I did research on premature infants in my first job as a psychology graduate student. I have continued that research to this day, when my daughter is taller and smarter than I am because we gave her touch therapy.

In the world of premature infants today, after they are out of medical jeopardy in the neonatal intensive care unit, they move to what is called the growing unit, where they are to grow enough to be discharged and taken home by their parents. We first tried to make premature infants grow by having them suck on pacifiers while they were being tube-fed. Then, thanks to research by our colleague Dr. Gene Anderson, which suggested that a lamb given a pacifier to suck on while receiving a tube thrives better than one not sucking on a pacifier during tube feeding,[1] we subsequently tried pacifiers with premature babies. We found that infants given pacifiers during their tube feedings gained more weight, went off tube feedings earlier, did better on newborn behavior and neurological examinations, and were discharged earlier, at a much lower hospital cost,[2] than infants not given pacifiers.

At the time of this study, we thought those babies given pacifiers might have gained more weight because they might be sleeping more and thus saving more calories by being less active. But they were not any less active, nor were they sleeping more. Although we did not know *why* the pacifier worked, it did work, and we reasoned that, if we stimulated even more areas on their bodies, the infants might gain even more weight. Several people had previously tried to give babies extra touch therapy, but the babies had not shown any growth gains, possibly because the researchers were touching too lightly and to the babies it felt like an unwelcome tickle stimulus. We began to massage babies from head to foot (all but their chests and stomachs; they did not want to be touched there, most likely because that was where all the tubes had been inserted, which the infants learned did not feel good). The babies who were massaged gained 47 percent more weight than those not massaged, a clearly significant weight gain.[3]

At the same time that we were massaging infants, our collaborator, Dr. Saul Schanberg from Duke University, was conducting studies on mother rats and rat pups. He found that the pups failed to thrive—and, in fact, died—when they were deprived of tongue-licking touch from their mother[4] (tongue licking is the primary way that mother rats touch their pups). Another colleague, Dr. Jeannie Brooks-Gunn, reported these remarkable findings to Jim Burke at Johnson & Johnson, who then invited us to share our findings with his company, which had just launched a mother-baby love campaign. Jim Burke understood the healing power of touch and commented that he believed loving touch could not only save the world from disease, but also from future war. His vision was shared by others at Johnson & Johnson, including Bob Rock, who had conducted the roundtables on touch there, and Jim Dettre, who had done most of the groundwork for implementing touch research. In addition, the well-known pediatrician T. Berry Brazelton and his close collaborator Ed Tronick were both very enthusiastic about touch research. They were present at several meetings to design the world's first Touch Research Institute.

Despite the fact that touch is the largest sense organ (because the skin is the largest organ in the body), it is the one most taken for granted and the one most overlooked when it comes to research efforts. Several other research institutes study vision, hearing, smell, and taste, but now, thanks to a seed grant from Jim Burke and Julia Freedman at Johnson & Johnson, as well as funding from various federal agencies and private corporations, we have established the Touch Research Institutes as multidisciplinary, multiuniversity faculties in four different places (the University of Paris, Philippines Medical Center, and the UCLA and University of Miami schools of medicine). To date, the institutes have conducted ninety-three separate studies on touch and touch therapies.

Although the many therapeutic benefits of touch have become increasingly clear—benefits such as decreases in stress and anxiety and their behavioral and biochemical manifestations, and the positive effects that touch has on growth, brain waves, breathing, heart rate, even the immune system—we still have the very large problem of minimal touch in our society. A study we conducted on touch in preschool nurseries revealed that children under the age of five were being touched less than 12 percent of the time, even in model nursery schools.[5] If touch is as critical for growth, development, and health as it appears to be in our studies, then our society has a big problem, long in the making, that we must address and overcome if we are to go forward in a healthy, loving way.

This book, about the importance of touch and touch therapy for our health, development, and well-being, and for the good of our culture, is our contribution toward that end. The first three chapters focus on the sociology and anthropology of touching and the basic psychophysical properties of touch. The remaining five chapters describe recent research on the value of touch therapies for everyone, from asthmatics to autistic children, from cancer patients to those with eating disorders.

Our research on the benefits gained from touch and touch therapy was the impetus for this book. Our intent was to share our firsthand knowledge of the important role that touch plays in our lives and to try and reverse the minimal-touch problem that keeps us from fully experiencing its many benefits.

Physicians regularly ask us how prolonged the effects of massage therapy are, and we have to respond that we could no more expect long-term effects if the massages were stopped than we could expect long-term effects of dieting if the dieting was stopped. Like diet and exercise, people may need a daily dose of touch.

Touch

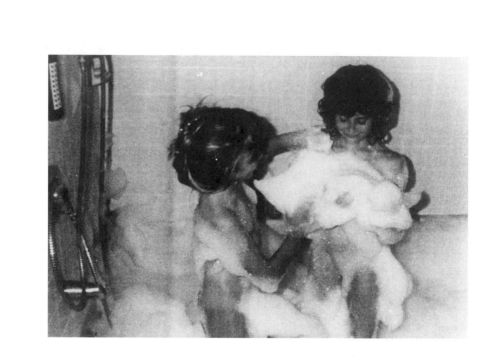

1

Touch Hunger

Tana was raised in a Romanian orphanage. At age seven, relief workers found her all skin and bones and only half the height of a normal child her age.[1] As with the many other children in the orphanage, her plight made the relief workers feel they were witnessing a cruel joke being played on these little survivors. Because there were so many children and the orphanage was so severely understaffed, Tana and the others had spent most of their time in cribs, and had been touched and held only during infrequent caregiving activities. Barely able to walk on their stick-like legs, the children stared at the recently arrived massage therapists and winced at their touch. But, after many months of regular nutrition and massage therapy, Tana (like the others who received the same treatment) was no longer a gaunt little skeleton, and her legs were strong enough for her to run without her toppling over.

The experience of Tana and the other Romanian orphans reinforces the critical importance of touch for growth and development. During and after World War II, similarly orphaned infants and children in overcrowded institutions were only rarely and briefly touched by nurses; without being affectionately held, hugged, and stroked, many of these infants died.

The Taboos against Touch

Amazingly, at the same time that American television viewers were cringing at the sight of the Romanian orphans, American teachers were being instructed not to touch their students for fear of sexual abuse lawsuits. Teachers now are no longer allowed to hug grade-schoolers if they do well in class, or pick up preschoolers when they fall on the playground. Even in our own university "model" preschool, we found that teachers were touching the one-year-olds less than 12 percent of the time.[2]

Schools have implemented several hundred child-abuse prevention programs costing millions of dollars, and millions of young children have participated in these programs. Typically, the programs give lessons on recognizing different kinds of touch, from "good" to "bad," telling the children how to say "No!" and how to get away, teaching which body parts are private, and teaching that any touch that does not feel good is "bad touch." Although everyone agrees it is important for children to be educated about "good touch/bad touch," or appropriate and inappropriate touch, it is depressing to see a three-year-old child wiggling free from a hugging teacher, saying, "Don't touch me. My mommy told me teachers can't touch me."

In the United States, National Public Radio (NPR) included a special program in their daily *Morning Edition* (1994) newscast, titled "Day Care Center Goes to Extremes to Protect Reputation." This story described how a daycare center constrained its staff from touching children. The director of the daycare said, "It's against our policy to pick up the kids. It's against our policy to hold them on our lap. The 'no-touch' policy is more to protect the center than the children. It would be too easy for one innocent hug or playful piggyback ride to be misinterpreted."

Other "no-touch" procedures include installing videocameras in classrooms and holding in-service sessions on "good touch/bad touch" for teachers, telling them how they can appropriately hold children on their lap. When asked at one of these sessions how they think they can touch children, teachers themselves gave the following examples: holding hands, arm around shoulder, hugging, patting on the back, holding hands on fieldtrips, holding the children during separations from parents, cuddling them when they're upset, giving first aid, giving arrival and departure hugs and high-fives, dressing, feeding, and toileting the children, patting their heads in recognition or praise, touching them for behavior or safety management, and removing any child who poses a danger to others. All these are considered acceptable forms of touch.

Other directives include never touching private areas (those a bathing suit would cover), always hugging from the side (avoiding frontal hugs), and never being alone with a child. Men are not allowed to change diapers, so men are not hired as daycare teachers. All daycare workers are fingerprinted and checked for criminal records. Yet, despite all these mandates, child abuse by daycare workers is on the increase.

A recent Oprah Winfrey show focused on this issue of teachers touching children. The president of the National Education Association said, "Our slogan is, teach, don't touch." One of the teachers on the show taught music. In the green room before the show, she told me that of course she had to touch children, as for example when she taught them the violin. But on the air she said, "In my classroom, we hug with our eyes." Oprah walked over to her and said, "Did you get that hug I just sent you?"

Sexual abuse is relatively rare in U.S. schools. As little as 1 percent of all reported sexual abuse cases involving children occur in schools, whereas ninety percent of abusive incidents involve parents and relatives. Nonetheless, school directors are spending more money on liability than on teacher salaries, and an increasing number of caregivers are leaving the childcare profession. This is a significant problem, because 50 percent of working women who are new mothers are back at work before their infant is one year old, and 60 percent of women with preschool children are working mothers. The Bureau of Labor estimated that in the year 2000, women accounted for approximately two-thirds of the expected new workers. Their children entered a daycare system where teachers were mandated not to touch children.

Despite the infrequency of sexual abuse cases in schools, schools have become a primary target for antitouch laws. More and more states are making it illegal for teachers to touch students, and even in those states that have not outlawed touch in schools, it is increasingly risky for teachers to touch students. Similarly, codes of ethics forbid touching by psychotherapists and counselors. Can you imagine a therapist counseling a hospice patient without being able to touch her or him? These laws are not just made to protect the child and the psychotherapy patient; they also benefit the insurance business.

Laws regarding touch exist for students as well as teachers. Behaviors once considered mere "teasing" are now reclassified as sexual harassment. And, although the laws do not require schools to teach about sexual harassment, children as young as six can be held legally responsible for it. In September 1996, six-year-old Jonathan Prevett, a first grade student at Southwest Elementary in Lexington, North Carolina, was accused of sexual harassment by a school official and barred from class for a day. Jonathan's "sexual harassment" had consisted of planting a kiss on his schoolmate's cheek. (His parents were offered $100,000 for the movie rights, which they declined.)

At school, teenagers also suffer the loss of touch from adults when they are deprived of their coaches' affectionate hugs and rubdowns for cold muscles. That may be the reason more teenagers are seen hugging their peers in school halls, grabbing whatever touch they can get as they pass from classroom to classroom. It may also be why sexual promiscuity and teenage pregnancy are on the increase, and could even explain the increasing incidence of eating disorders and addictive behaviors. Meanwhile, although "no touch" mandates are intended to decrease child abuse and sex abuse, negative forms of touch have increased and discipline "in loco parentis" (the teacher's right to spank the child) has not yet disappeared in all states. "No touch" mandates do not seem to make those negative behaviors go away, as is evidenced by increasingly frequent reports of child abuse in the press.

The Critical Importance of Touch

Bumper stickers that ask, "Have you hugged your child today?" are disappearing as parents become wary of touching their own children. This behavior, reminiscent of an earlier, more formal time, is not a good idea, because children need touch for survival. Their growth and development thrive on touch. And how will they learn about love and affection if not through touch?

There are other, fortunate societies where touch and familial bonding still exist (figure 1.1). Studies in Uganda show that babies carried in upright positions are quicker to walk and faster to develop in other areas as well (figure 1.2). This upright

Figure 1.1
Panamanian mother breastfeeding infant.

Figure 1.2
African mother carrying child.

position heightens the babies' visual alertness while it helps develop their back and neck muscles. Carried around all day, these Ugandan babies become familiar with the world as they view it from their secure vantage point. Because they are held close and upright, they stay calmer; studies show they even cry less than babies who are not carried regularly. This closeness is also evident in numerous other countries, including India, where the whole family sleeps on large palm mats on the floor or on several cots in one small room, and Japan where Japanese infants share their parents' futons.

In all of these countries massage is also used as a familial, nurturant routine. Massages are likely to nurture the parent as much as, or more than the infant, but in some places some parents are afraid of their children's young, vulnerable bodies. Other parents are afraid to touch their children because they feel that their natural sensual desire to touch their offspring may be construed as sexual. But often, massaging their infants helps both mothers and fathers feel closer to their children in ways they otherwise could not. Massaging also allows parents to know their child's body better, and imparts the message to the child that touch is good.

Touch in Everyday Activities

Touch is the first sense to develop, and it functions even after seeing and hearing begin to fade.[3] Infants and young children are dependent on touch for learning about the world. During the first year of life, everything goes in the mouth and is learned through the mouth's touching.[4] The young child explores the physical world by touch and learns the many facets it can convey, including elasticity, resilience, shape, sharpness, softness, temperature, and texture. Children learn about general hygiene, grooming, and the properties of matter from the sense of touch. They also learn safety and self-preservation, such as how to avoid frostbite, hot stoves, noxious substances, and prickers, and they learn how to write, receiving hand-over-hand assistance in penmanship class.

For the same reasons, touch is critical for adults. I will never forget how grateful I was that I could *feel* our electric blanket when it caught fire one night as our baby daughter was lying between me and my husband. Touch is also critical for most people's work. Imagine a world of computers without touch, or imagine being a potter, a surgeon, a painter, or a fisherman without touch. The world-renowned cellist Jacqueline Du Pré lost all sensation in her hands one night during a concert and had to guide her fingers with her eyes to get through her performance; she subsequently died of multiple sclerosis, a progressive disease that robs its victims, mostly women, of touch. Touch becomes even more critical when the other senses break down. For example, tactile vocoders are being developed for deaf children to hear by touch, and a vibrating tactile language called "Vibrates" is being developed for blind adults to read with their fingertips, as they now do with the raised Braille dots.

In addition to being critical for growth and development, communication and learning, touch also serves to comfort and give reassurance and self-esteem. A child's first emotional bonds are built from physical contact, laying the foundation for further emotional and intellectual development.

Despite the many critically important functions of touch, most children, in our country at least, are socialized at an early age to limit their touching. They are scolded when touching their own body parts and are admonished not to touch the bodies of others (as well as many objects in the environment).[5] By adolescence, they have learned to be cautious about physical intimacy and to express themselves by facial expressions and words rather than by touch. Curiously, however, as adults we talk about touch in many personal and sentimental ways. We say, "Your words have touched me deeply," or "She has a soft touch," or "He was a bit touchy." In such advertising slogans as "Reach out and touch someone" (AT&T), or "Touch their todays. Touch their tomorrows" (Johnson & Johnson), we use the term rather freely, but these appealing words are rarely translated into action.

Americans, who are among the world's least tactile people, limit their touching to family members and sexual intimates. With this in mind, imagine being alone in a hospital without a family member around to hold your hand. "Fifteen days in a hospital without touch" was the reason one patient recently gave for escaping and walking home from a local hospital in his pajamas and hospital wristband. Still worse, imagine being a senior citizen (and particularly an articulate older man) confined to bed rest in a nursing home. Older men are touched even less than older women in nursing homes. Some suggested this happens because men discourage touching; they are not accustomed to being touched by their inferiors, and they consider caregivers their inferiors.[6] Some senior citizens have fared better because they have pets and have been able to give them the fondling and cuddling that they missed from people. In return, these older pet owners had less cardiovascular disease and lived longer than those without pets.[7]

Our bodies have eighteen square feet of skin, which makes skin our largest sense organ.[3] Because skin cannot shut its eyes or cover its ears, it is in a constant state of readiness to receive messages—it is always on. The first sensory input in life comes from the sense of touch while still in the womb, and touch continues to be the primary means of experiencing the world throughout infancy and well into childhood, even into aging.

Touch across Cultures and Species

Touch, more than any other sense, is universal across cultures and species. Most animals know that touch is critical to life (figure 1.3). Rat pups do not survive without their mother rat's tongue-licking touch.[8] Monkeys huddle in a corner when they are touch-deprived. Animals such as the rat and the monkey are dependent on the parents' touch to grow and develop, much like people. On the negative side of touch, mother goats will abandon their young if the baby goat gets touched by another animal or a human.

Many human cultures know the primary value of touch. In African cultures, for example, people live skin-to-skin with virtually everyone (figure 1.4). They start very early, passing their babies from person to person, no matter their age.[9] Some cultures do more touching than others. For example, the French touch people more than the Americans or the British.[10] They are not discreet about their lovemaking, as I recently learned

Figure 1.3
Sea lions frolicking on the Galapagos.

Figure 1.4
African children holding their siblings.

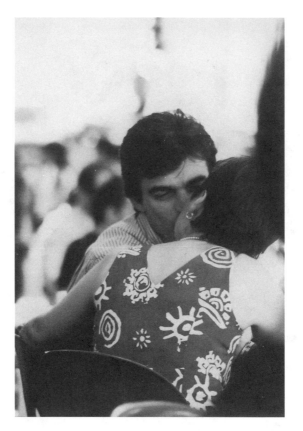

Figure 1.5
French couple kissing.

while walking through the Luxembourg Gardens (figure 1.5).
In broad daylight on a Sunday, when fathers and children were
there in great numbers to sail their boats in the garden's pond,
a young couple wedged into only one chair were managing to
do what an American couple would only do in the dark in a
more private place. From the very early age of the preschool
years, the French are touched more. According to one of our
studies, French mothers observed at McDonald's in Paris touch

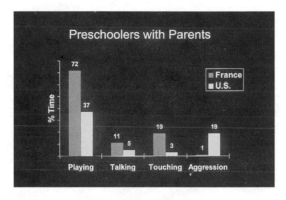

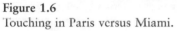

Figure 1.6
Touching in Paris versus Miami.

their preschoolers more than American mothers at McDonald's in Miami do (figure 1.6). Also, and possibly related, French children are less aggressive toward other children on the playground than their American counterparts are.[11] And, whereas teenagers at McDonald's in Paris touch *each other* more, our study found that teenagers at McDonald's in Miami touch *themselves* (like self-hugging and playing with their hair) more. The French teenagers are also less aggressive with each other.[12]

The "laying-on of hands" has a long tradition, extending beyond recorded history, and has been a symbol of power in many cultures. As far back as 1553 B.C., the Ebers Papyrus showed the early practice of healing by touch.[13] In ancient Greece, the god of healing was Asclepius (son of Apollo) who, according to myth, healed people by simply touching them. In the Greece of Hippocrates' time, around 400 B.C., there were hand healers (comparable to today's internists) called *kheirourgos*. This is the origin of the word "surgeon," even though the *kheirourgos* used the palm and their fingers, rather than surgical methods, to heal. One of the most famous

Roman healers, Galen (A.D. 130), used massage as a medical treatment.

In all four gospels of the New Testament, the laying-on of hands is commonplace for children, lepers, and those afflicted with disease. The practice was dropped from the church during the seventeenth century, but the use of the custom by royalty continued. Almost all the monarchs of France and England exercised the royal touch, using it to treat many diseases;[14] the practice continued into modern times. In France, as late as 1825, Charles X touched between 120 and 130 people.

The laying-on of royal hands was frequently associated with scrofula, which came to be known as the "King's Evil." In 1712, Samuel Johnson contracted scrofula from his wet nurse. When he was two and a half, his mother took him to London, where he was among the 200 people touched by Queen Anne— in his case, without being cured. This queen was the last royal figure in England to perform the healing gesture.

In an attempt to determine why the healing touch worked, the eighteenth-century Austrian physician Franz Mesmer conducted some studies in Paris that led him to suggest a magnetic fluid emanating from the body transferred healing energy from one person to another. Mesmer, who sought to treat disease through animal magnetism, subsequently developed mesmerism, a therapeutic application of hypnotism.

Why did touch healing fall out of favor? Touch researchers offer several possible reasons, including sexual taboos and the development of drugs and treatment technologies that dramatically changed the field of medicine. In his book *Touching Is Healing*, Jules Older claims, "Touch has become taboo and that is the reason it does not appear in medical textbooks or curricula."[15] Older elaborates on this with an example from psychiatry:[15] Karl Menninger, one of the world's renowned psychoanalytic theorists, suggested that analysts should not shake hands with their patients. Indeed, most practitioners do not advocate excessive contact between therapist and patient; however, Menninger did not distinguish between therapeutic, sexual, and aggressive touch. All types of touch seemed to be, in his words, the "mark of a ruthless criminal." In that light, it is interesting to note that a decade ago, touch was most often associated with sexuality, but today, in our litigious society, it is more associated with criminality in increasingly frequent court cases on sexual harassment and sexual abuse.

As Freudian psychoanalysis (which discourages touch) is waning, doctors are becoming more willing to touch their patients. Some medical schools, such as Duke and Harvard, have even included touching as part of their medical school curriculum. Alternative treatments such as massage therapy and acupuncture are also helping to bring touch therapy back to medicine, where since prerecorded time it legitimately reigned as the primary form of therapy.

The advent of drugs was also a problem that negatively affected touch healing. As Voltaire said, "Physicians pour drugs, about which they know little, to cure diseases, about which they know less, into humans, about whom they know nothing."[16] Drugs can either heighten sensitivity to touch or deaden the sense of touch. Stimulants, including amphetamines, cocaine, and caffeine, increase arousal, as indicated by increased heart rate and blood pressure, alertness, and confidence. They also slow down blood circulation, leaving a person feeling cold and jumpy to the touch. Depressants, including barbiturates, narcotics, and tranquilizers, dull the sense of touch. Muscle relaxants, tranquilizers, and sleep-inducers such as Quaaludes break down inhibitions, but also tend to make people less sensitive to touch, as does alcohol, which can depress the system and its touch sensitivity. The only depressant drug that seems to enhance touch is marijuana, although heightened sensitivity to touch depends on the person's state of mind before taking the marijuana. Among other environmental negative aspects for touch are cold or muggy weather. Warm baths and waterbeds, on the other hand, can enhance touch sensitivity.

As most critics suggest, the medical profession focuses on treatment rather than prevention.[13] A doctor's training focuses on dealing with a disease, generally through drug therapy. Little emphasis is put on maintaining health. As Norman Cousins so succinctly wrote, "The physician celebrates computerized tomography. The patient celebrates the outstretched hand."[17]

Although touch is an effective healing agent, it is underutilized by healing practitioners, from neurologists to social workers, and has been generally ignored by institutions and neglected by researchers.[17] Jules Older's data suggest that

Of one hundred patients walking into a doctor's office, only fifty will have an identifiable physical ailment. Of this fifty, thirty-five will have a self-limiting disorder, an illness or injury which will get better by itself, with or without the doctor's treatment. Of the other fifty patients who come to the door—these are the ones without evidence of pathology—five will be there for administrative reasons (such as an insurance claim or a certificate of disability), and another ten for preventive measures (vaccination, contraception, diet advice). The remaining thirty-five seek help with life problems, usually of an emotional nature.[18]

Older highlights the point that most patients are seeking contact and a little reassurance that could be helped by a doctor's caring touch.

More recently, a 1993 U.S. Public Health Survey estimated that 70 to 80 percent of Americans who visit conventional physicians suffer from a stress-related disorder. As Dr. Lynn Carmichael, chairman of the University of Miami Department of Family Medicine, says, "The good doctor is a good groomer."[18] Joan Carmichael, a fellow researcher in that department, concurs, saying, "Laying-on of hands is not merely folklore or mysticism. Reinstituting the backrub as standard hospital procedure could balance the introduction of the computerized axial tomography scanner."[13]

Older relates an interesting anecdote about an osteopath who had a habit of playfully pinching an older patient's big toe during his examination. The patient says, "I've been waiting for you, to tell you it is because of you I am still alive." The osteopath says, "What are you talking about?" "Well," says the older man, "every morning you pinched my toe when the others weren't looking." The physician, puzzled, says, "Yes, but what does that have to do with . . ." The patient interrupts, saying, "Nobody plays with the toes of dying men. So I decided I must not be dying after all."[19] The doctor's touch let this man know he was still a viable human being.

Touch, affecting both tactile and pressure receptors, stimulates the central nervous system into a state of relaxation. Anxiety and stress levels, both behavioral and biochemical, are then reduced and the general effect is a relaxed, more attentive state. But there are also specific effects, such as reduced pain for those with arthritis, increased peak air flow for those with asthma, and increased natural killer cell activity for the HIV patient.[20] The anecdotal and research data on these and the many other positive effects of touch—all detailed in these chapters—will serve to remind us just how vital touch is and how it needs to be a greater part of our lives.

2

Touch as Communication

Touch is our most social sense. Unlike seeing, hearing, smelling, and tasting, which can generally be done alone, touching typically implies an interaction with another person. Although touch is extremely important for social interactions, the term is rarely used in books on communication skills. Nonetheless, many research studies conducted on touch as communication have focused on how it varies widely by gender, age, class, and culture.

Cultural Differences

Touching is usually an intimate act that, according to Ashley Montagu, is only practiced between people of the same culture or class. Cultural differences in touching have been widely reported.[1] As mentioned earlier, we observed the differences between French and American children on playgrounds with their parents and peers.[2] The American parents watched and touched their children less than the French parents. The American children played with their parents less, talked with and touched their parents less, and were more aggressive toward their parents than the French children. During peer interactions, the American children also showed less touching of their peers but more grabbing their peers' toys, more aggression toward their peers, and more fussing.

In another study, we observed adolescents at McDonald's restaurants in Paris and Miami to assess the amount of touching and aggression that took place during peer interactions.[3] The American adolescents spent less time leaning against, stroking, kissing, and hugging their peers than their French counterparts. Instead, they showed more self-touching and more aggressive verbal and physical behavior.

Some of these differences may relate to differences in early touch exposure. An American child may become more active and vocal and a Japanese child more passive and quiet because of the different kinds of touch they experience from their mothers. From the beginning of life, the kind of touch a child receives—calming/soothing stroking in the case of Japanese infants, and more abrupt, arousing, tapping-and-poking touch in the case of American infants—may explain some of the differences in the children's later behavior.[4] For example, Japanese children have constant physical contact with their parents. The relationship between them is sometimes called "skinship." Because of this sustained dependence of the child upon the mother, the child becomes identified as a member of a group rather than as an independent person.

It is interesting that, in touching cultures, adult aggression is low, whereas in cultures in which touch is limited, adult aggression is high.[5] A classic example comes from Margaret Mead's work on the Arapesh and the Mundugamoor of New Guinea.[6] The Arapesh infants are always carried in a small net bag by the mother, which allows the child to experience constant physical contact and on-demand breastfeeding with the mother. The adults in that society are nonaggressive, gentle people, and warfare is not practiced. By contrast, within the same country, the Mundugamoor are a relatively aggressive, warring people whose infants are carried in a basket suspended from the mother's forehead, out of contact with the mother's body. Like the Arapesh, the !Kung babies of the Kalahari in Africa are in constant skin-to-skin contact with their mothers. They ride in soft leather slings on the mothers' side and receive lots of handling and kissing from older children. They too grow up to be a very peaceful people.[7]

Early experiences with touch also seem to affect greeting behaviors in different cultures. Those that have more contact with infants also make more contact during their greetings. According to a long list compiled by Ashley Montagu, this includes nose rubbing, embracing, kissing, cheek-tweaking, hair-mussing, and even back-slapping.[8] Australian friends are known to kiss, shake hands, and even sometimes cry over one another.[9] Moroccans join their hands together with a quick motion, then immediately separate them and kiss their own hand. Andaman Islanders in the Bay of Bengal regularly greet each other by sitting down on the lap of the other, with their arms around each other's necks, weeping and wailing for two or three minutes, until they are tired.[10] Brothers, father and son, mother and son, mother and daughter, and even husband and wife greet each other this way, with the husband sitting on his wife's lap. When Andaman friends leave each other, one of them lifts the hand of the other to his mouth and gently blows on it. The French, at least the Parisian French, used to greet each other by a kiss on each cheek. Now they kiss the cheeks three times alternately; with more familiar people, they add a fourth kiss. These very physical greetings are a dramatic contrast to the typically stiff handshake that Americans use for greetings.

Even a handshake, though, is subject to social and cultural differences. In her book *The Magic of Touch*, Sherrie Cohen notes that "the handshake is the caveman's legacy to subsequent generations. It is an example of touch, not only as contact, but also as contract—a touch that says we are equal here and we can trust each other."[11] She describes a number of different types of handshakes, including the "gloveshake," otherwise known as the politician's handshake, where the politician encircles the shaker's hand with his or her two hands. There are the "knuckle grinders" (tough guys), "stiff-armers" (those who want to keep you at a distance), and "upper arm grabbers" (more power plays), as well as the "body lowerers" (those who bow as if shaking hands with royalty). Clearly the "wet noodle" handshake will not conquer the world and the "knuckle grinder" will not win friends.

Hugs are similarly variable. The *Daddy's Hug Book* has pictures that illustrate the many kinds of hugs, most of which might as well be a stiff handshake. In the "A frame" hug, the partners' rear ends stick out to form the A frame, and in the "baby burp" hug, the back-thumping does not exactly look affectionate. Try to imagine the variety of hugs there must have been when 15,000 people came together years ago on the University of Southern California campus to form the world's largest hug. How these customs evolve is not clear, but children become accustomed to certain kinds of contact at a very early age, from being carried in an infant seat in the United States to being in a body sling in the Kalahari.

Sidney Jourard, a University of Florida psychologist, visited cafés in different parts of the world and recorded the number of times two people who were sharing coffee touched each other.[12] In London, the tally was 0; in Gainesville, Florida, 2; in Paris 110; and in San Juan, Puerto Rico, more than 180. Most sociologists would agree that societies like those in the Mediterranean countries (Spain, France, Italy, Greece, Turkey, Egypt, for example) are contact societies, whereas the more northern societies in countries such as Holland, Great Britain, and the United States are not.

Some suggest that the amount of contact generally relates to religious practices, such that people in Great Britain and the United States, for example, engage in less contact because of their puritanical, Protestant backgrounds. But touch behavior does not strictly follow from the political or religious beliefs prevalent in the country. If it did, then people in religious countries like Italy and Greece might be more physically inhibited. But the opposite seems true, because the Greeks and Italians are among the most touching people in the world. Strangers entering a Greek home are welcomed with a warm embrace and kisses on the cheek, and Italians are world-renowned touchers. People in Sweden, whose liberal attitudes toward sexuality would seem to defy Protestant strictures, at least in the religious sense, are relatively inhibited about touch, and touch gestures such as embracing or hanging on each others' shoulders are unusual.

According to Ashley Montagu, "England is a land full of peculiar people, of people who are adults, who seldom touch each other, and in which one apologizes to one's father or one's mother when one touches them accidentally. This, of course, was a rule in well-bred families which means more care in breeding horses than care in breeding children."[13]

The physician P. N. K. Heylings wrote an article in the *British Medical Journal* entitled, "The No Touching Epidemic—an English Disease."[14] The symptoms he describes include feelings of loneliness and isolation, doubts about other people's loyalties, feelings of insecurity, emotional inhibitions, unusual reactions both to being inadvertently touched and to touching others, inability to communicate with people standing nearby, and antagonism to massages as a form of therapy.

Other observational studies to determine the effects of touch on public behavior have been conducted in New England. In one study, shoppers were touched by a salesman offering pizza samples.[15] The customers who were touched were more influenced by the salesperson, they liked that person more, and more of them felt the salesperson liked them more. Similarly, in a restaurant, waitresses were asked to touch the diners as they returned the diners' change.[16] Diners who were touched left higher tips, even though they did not rate the quality of the food or service any differently from those who were not touched. In still another study, librarians were asked to alternately touch and not touch the hands of students as they checked out their books.[17] Those students who were touched reported more positive feelings about the library, even though the touch only lasted a half-second, and half the students did not even remember being touched. The touch, however, had different effects on male and female students. Women responded favorably to the touch, but men responded with ambivalence. Those men who had been touched by same-sex librarians were particularly negative in their reactions.

Sex Differences

Sex differences frequently emerge in studies on touch. In a hospital study, 85 percent of the touched patients, but only 53 percent of the untouched patients, responded positively about the hospital and its personnel; those touched apparently recuperated faster. However, in a more carefully controlled study by the researchers Fisher and Gallant,[18] the report also included the sex of the person being touched. Women who were touched reported less anxiety concerning surgery than women who were not touched, but men who were touched reported more anxiety. The touched women also reached out and touched the nurse's hand more than the men did, and tended to have lower blood pressures in the recovery room, whereas the touched men had higher readings. The researchers suggested that being touched might make men feel more vulnerable and more dependent.

Men and women may react to touch differently because they have been socialized differently. Ashley Montagu suggests that women are often considered and treated as inferiors to men, so they are touched more than men.[2] A study by S. M. Jourard revealed that female infants were more frequently touched by both parents than male infants, and that daughters later touched both parents more than sons did.[12] In another study by Jourard and Rubin, both mothers and fathers touched their daughters in more regions of their bodies than they did their sons, and the daughters in turn touched their parents in more of these areas than sons did.[12] It is conceivable that later gender differences could result from these early differences in touch. We know that touch-deprived animals become more aggressive, so the more aggressive behavior noted in boys might derive from their being touched less often by their parents.

Even greater gender differences have been noted among adults. Studies by the researcher Nancy Henley found that men touch women more frequently than women touch men, most likely because men are typically higher status.[19] This pecking-order mentality is probably why older men are touched less often than women in nursing homes. Henley found that when women had more status, they were more likely to initiate the touching.

These differences might also relate to women being touched more often by a variety of people (mother, father, same/opposite-sex friends) than men, and also to their having more exposure to touch in medical situations, as for example during routine gynecology examinations. For this reason, touch could be reassuring for women in hospitals, but disruptive for men who have less experience with touch in general, and especially in medical situations. Another possibility relates to the female patients being touched by a same-sex nurse (most hospital nurses are females), whereas the male patients are touched by an opposite-sex person. Men in this situation might misinterpret the touch as sexual in nature, even though other data suggest that touches on the hand and the shoulder are usually interpreted as nonsexual. Still another possibility is that the men view the female nurses as lower status. As previously noted, people of a higher status are more likely to touch people of a lower status than vice versa, and some people who view themselves as higher status may be offended by lower-status people touching them.

The status hypothesis comes from a number of studies by researcher Henley.[19] In many public, nonintimate settings such as shopping centers, a bank, and a university campus, men touched women more than women touched men. In addition, touch from older to younger people was more frequent than touch from younger to older. Also, touch from those in higher income groups to those of lower status was more frequent than from lower to higher. But those findings were only seen in impersonal public settings. In more intimate circumstances, touch does not differ by sex. Brenda Major found that in more intimate greeting/leavetaking situations in such places as airports, there were no sex differences.[20] Men were not more likely to be the initiators of touch and women the recipients. Opposite-sex touch occurred more frequently than same-sex touch. Female-female and male-male touch were about equal to each other. During the same study, touch observations involving children suggested that girls initiated touch more than boys and were more often the recipients of touch from everyone but boys.

To determine where people touched each other, Jourard used a drawing of the body divided into eleven areas, front and back, and observed where friends touched them (figure 2.1).[12] The hands, forearms, upper arms, shoulders, head, and forehead received more touch than other body parts. Again, however, there were sex differences. Women felt that any touch on their thighs, lips, or chest was sexual. Men perceived touching in those parts of the body as friendly, warm, and affectionate. These different interpretations of touch by the two sexes may partially explain why men are touched less by female nurses in hospital and nursing home settings.

These sex differences do not occur in preschool age children and, in a study in our preschool, we noted that girls and boys are touched by teachers and by other children predominantly on the same body parts, the hands, forearms, upper arms, shoulders, head, and forehead.[21] The power of touch for young children is illustrated in a study conducted by June Triplett and Sarah Arneson,[22] where preschool children in a pediatric ward were divided into two groups. One group was given *only* verbal comfort when they showed distress, and the other was given simultaneous verbal and tactile comfort, including holding, patting, rocking, stroking, and offering a pacifier. Only seven of the forty verbal comforts succeeded in quieting the children, but fifty-three of the sixty tactile-verbal comforts were successful.

Touch and Aging

Ashley Montagu wrote wisely about touch and the aging,[23]

Everyone wants to live long, but no one wants to grow old, for old age, as someone has aptly put it, is a dirty trick. The answer to that,

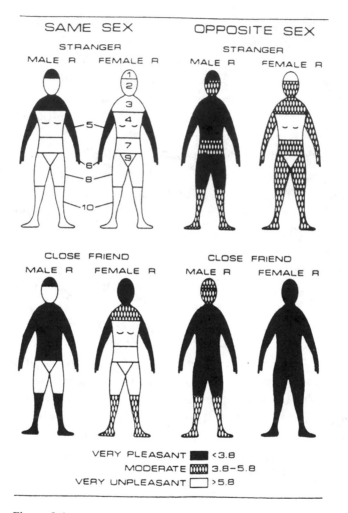

Figure 2.1
Sidney Jourard's diagram for coding body parts touched. From
Nguyen, T., Heslin, R., and Nguyen, M. L. (1975). The meanings of
touch: Sex differences. *Journal of Communication* 25: 92–103 and
Nonverbal Communication, *Sage's Annual Review of Communication*.

of course, is to die young—as late as possible. But that is mainly a matter of the spirit. In most cases, the body wears out long before we are ready to vacate the premises. . . . In the course of time, the skin changes in character, but the spirit within us is, like good wine, capable of improving with time. . . . Tactile needs do not seem to change with aging—if anything, they seem to increase.

Ironically, the older some people get, the more they want to be touched, but the opportunity to be touched by friends and family gets markedly reduced because many people do not like touching older people. Nursing students, for example, have considerable anxiety about touching older people.[24] Spouses are often separated from each other in nursing homes, which makes touching difficult, as do other obstacles like bedsides and poorly designed wheelchairs. These impediments highlight the need to provide older people in nursing homes with additional touch opportunities such as touch materials and objects to hold, children and pets for them to touch, massages, and dancing events where there is physical contact.

In *Touching for Pleasure*, Kennedy and Dean describe an incident involving two nursing home residents missing at the dinner hour that dramatically illustrates the problem of touch in older people.[25]

The alert spread quickly throughout the home, and the search began. All the rooms and beds were empty and the outdoor patio bare. A nurse checked to see if any medication was missing from the storage closet and, upon opening the door, screamed. She found the man and the woman. They were embracing in silence. She quickly called for security. The two "sex offenders" were separated and escorted to their rooms. Families were called, conferences held, and doctors consulted. The consensus was that the two promiscuous culprits should not be allowed further contact. Humiliated and confused, frightened and guilt-ridden, the two rapidly withdrew from friends and family. Within weeks of the crime, they both died.

Touch Therapies for Older People

A study by researchers O'Neil and Calhoun found a correlation between "sensory deficits" and senile traits such as irritability, forgetfulness, and careless grooming or eating habits among forty-two people age seventy or over living in a nursing home.[26] Those residents who received massages, frequent stroking, hugs, squeezes of the hands and arm, love pats on the cheek, and affectionate touches of their head showed fewer signs of senility. They were more alert, better humored, and more physically vital than those residents who were not frequently touched.

Gay Luce, who founded SAGE, a group dedicated to exploring the excitement of old age, teaches massage as one of the SAGE experiences.[27] She first shows older men and women how to massage themselves and then how to massage each other. Most of the eighty-year-olds she instructed thought that massaging each other was relaxing and comforting. Although there were some who had not been touched for years and who associated touch with their spouses, which made them feel tense and nostalgic, the majority found that this kind of touch was not threatening because it was predictable and very easy to learn. She also found that giving a backrub was often as satisfying as getting a backrub.

In another study, J. Lynch and his colleagues reported that older people who had pets outlived those who had no pets.[28] Stroking pets lowered people's blood pressure. Pet therapists are becoming a major commercial enterprise, and pets now receive therapy training almost as frequently as obedience training. Many pets who might otherwise be euthanized in an animal hospital, or who are unable to complete the "pets for blindness or handicapped" training, are placed in hospital settings, residential facilities, children's shelters, and nursing homes for the elderly. Pets are also used with children who are psychologically disturbed. Children on the psychiatric unit sleep better and are less depressed when they can play with pets, and playing with pets also helps children with cancer have less anticipatory nausea when they go for chemotherapy.

At the Touch Research Institutes, we recently conducted a study on touch for the aging, using infants as therapists instead of pets.[29] We compared "grandparent" volunteers massaging infants (figure 2.2) with "grandparent" volunteers being massaged themselves. Both experiences had positive effects, including such lifestyle changes as participants having more social contacts, drinking less coffee, and making fewer trips to the doctor's office. Also, both sets of volunteers had better sleeping patterns, less depression, and greater self-esteem.

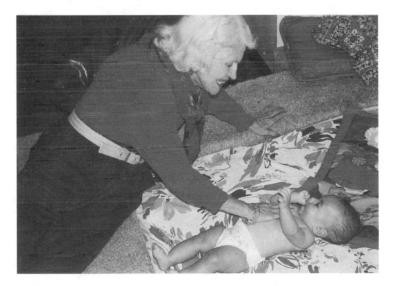

Figure 2.2
Volunteer "grandparent" massaging infant.

Surprisingly, the effects were greater when the volunteer grand-parents gave the massage than when they received the massage.

Sarah, one of the volunteer grandparents, told us, "Massaging babies has made me feel alive and young again." A retired pediatric nurse, Sarah had lost her husband several years before. She had grown children and grandchildren, but because they lived on the opposite coast, she was not only deprived of *being* touched, she also rarely got to touch her grandchildren, and no longer had the option of touching children that she formerly had on her job as a pediatric nurse. Massaging the infants not only gave her touch stimulation, but also gave her some time with grandchild-like children, and being able to care for children again helped increase her self-esteem.

3

Touch in Development

Touch in Early Development

Animal Handling

By looking at how animal mothers handle their offspring, we can learn a little of how important touch is for human babies. In several species, the mother's licking newborns is critical for the development of many systems in the baby animals, including the circulatory, digestive, gastrointestinal, genitourinary, immunological, neuroendocrine, reproductive, and respiratory systems. As already noted, if rat mothers do not lick their offspring, the rat pups will die. Rats, later in their development, provide their own stimulation by self-licking, as do cats and many other animals.

The importance of touch in infant development is highlighted by many handling experiments that mimic the mother's behavior. An experimental study conducted by S. Levine and his colleagues found that rats who were handled in infancy had higher levels of antibodies (cells that fight off infection) in their blood after immunization than those who were not handled,[1] indicating a link between early touch and the immune system. Other experiments showed greater weight gain, more activity, less fearfulness, and greater resistance to stress following extra handling. Similar studies in Victor Denenberg's lab suggested that rats handled during the first days of life weighed more, had better performance on cognitive tasks, and survived longer.[2] Still other studies by M. J. Meaney and his colleagues show that even memory is greater in aging rats who received more handling early in life.[3]

The rat is a good animal to study for touch-deprivation effects on people; both rats and people experience growth retardation if they are touch-deprived. Preliminary data from a recent magnetic resonance imaging study of preterm newborns by Neena Modi and her colleagues at Hammersmith Hospital in London suggest that the memory area of the brain (the hippocampus) might be more developed following massage. This also happens in rats. Researchers suggest the reason is that the extra pressure stimulation lowers cortisol levels (stress hormones), and lower stress hormone levels allow for greater nerve cell development in the hippocampus. The same may apply with a newborn baby; research done at the Touch Research Institutes[4] and by Neena Modi shows that cortisol levels decrease following a massage.[5] Whether there is less senility in people who received more touch early in life is still an open question,[3] nor do we yet know whether touch-deprivation effects can be reversed later in life. For example, the grandparent volunteers who were massaged and who massaged babies in the study described in the preceding chapter might have experienced improved memory, but we don't know if that is true or not because, unfortunately, we did not measure memory in that study. In this vein, however, several university computer centers have reported that a disproportionate number of their computer programmers come from India and can remember large mazes of numbers. This might relate to the widespread childrearing practice of providing two massages a day to babies in India.

Several decades ago Harry Harlow, at the University of Wisconsin, performed a classic experiment on touching monkeys.[6] He built one surrogate mother out of terry cloth and a second surrogate mother out of wire mesh. For some of the monkey infants, the terry-cloth mother provided milk and the wire mother did not. For others, the condition was reversed. The monkey infants preferred the cloth mother without the milk over the wire mother with milk, suggesting that they needed the touch stimulation as much as, if not more, than the nourishment.

Harlow's experiment demonstrated that contact with a terrycloth mother was more important to the infant than a wire mother that had a built-in feeding bottle. The infant monkeys would typically hang on to the cloth mother and then lean over and sip off the wire mother. Infant monkeys who had no real *or* surrogate mother developed patterns of clasping their own bodies. As these deprived monkeys grew older, they did not develop normal grooming patterns and had difficulty reproducing.

In our book *Touch in Early Development,*[7] Steve Suomi, one of Harlow's students who continued this research, wrote, "The history of interest in contact goes back to Harry Harlow who, over 30 years ago, alerted psychology and the rest of the sciences to the importance of touch by what he called contact comfort in his pioneering studies of infant monkeys reared on artificial surrogates."

In a later experiment, Suomi showed that touch was the critical stimulation the monkeys were missing in their mothers' absence.[7] By separating the mother and her infant with Plexiglas, the infant was still able to see, hear, and smell the mother, but not touch her. The infant monkeys did not fare well; their immune systems broke down. Fortunately for these monkeys,

Figure 3.1
Harry Harlow's peer-reared monkeys forming a "choo-choo" train.
From Suomi, S. J. (1995). Touch and the immune system in rhesus
monkeys. In Field, T. M. (ed.), *Touch in Early Development.*
Lawrence Erlbaum, 89–103.

having peer monkeys for comfort helped make them normal
again (figure 3.1).

Touch during Pregnancy, Labor, and Delivery

Early contact starts from the beginning of pregnancy. Pregnant
women often apply massage oil on their abdomen to prevent
stretch marks after birth. Midwives also encourage massaging
the area around the opening to the vagina, which is stretched
and often torn during delivery. Natural childbirth classes teach
women's partners to massage them during labor to help circulation, contraction of the uterus, and removal of the placenta.
The fetuses might feel this stimulation and respond as they
do to vibrating devices, according to researchers in the United
States and France who recorded fetal activity in response to

vibrating devices, suggesting that the fetus perceives the vibration.[8] (We have also noted recently that very young fetuses increase their activity in response to our massaging their mothers' feet.) Animal researchers have expressed concern about parents using vibrating devices because they negatively affect the developing auditory system in fetal chicks, but on the plus side, the slow, rhythmic movement of a massage with a vibrating device would probably just move the amniotic fluid around a little more than usual—and those fetuses might even turn into good swimmers.

The fetus gets a continuous massage for the entire nine months, both from the amniotic fluid and from the mother's "insides." In addition, a pregnant woman naturally massages her baby in the womb. If the baby pushes, the mother might push back, or playfully poke a bit, and this way she and the baby develop a relationship. The infant feels the motions of the mother's hands, and begins to become familiar with his or her mother's caress. Touch alters oxytocin (an estrogen-dependent chemical), which relaxes the individual, promotes touch, encourages bonding, triggers milk letdown during breastfeeding, and sets off the uterine contractions that accompany childbirth (and orgasm).[9]

In one of our studies, twenty-six pregnant women were assigned to a massage therapy or relaxation therapy group for five weeks.[10] Both groups reported feeling less anxious after the first session and less leg pain after the first and last session. Only the massage therapy group, however, reported reduced anxiety, improved mood, better sleep, and less back pain by the last day of the study. In addition, the massage therapy group had decreased uterine stress-hormone (norepinephrine) levels. They also had fewer complications during labor, their infants had fewer postnatal complications, and fewer of their infants were born prematurely.

Unfortunately, the massage stops after delivery unless the parents know the importance of infant massage. In his book *Birth Without Violence*, Frederick Leboyer tried to describe birth through the eyes of the infant.[11] As a result of what he learned, he changed the way he delivered babies: he dimmed the lights, lowered the noise levels, and massaged and bathed the newborn in warm water.

The infant's breathing is helped by the massaging action of uterine contractions and the passage through the birth canal. The four-inch passage through the birth canal is both a human being's most "dangerous journey in life" and the "best massage in life." Without the massaging activity of the movement through the birth canal, the infant's respiration system may develop more slowly. For example, prematurely born, cesarean-delivered infants can have respiratory problems. Knowing this, doctors often perform stress tests before cesareans to determine whether the baby's respiratory system is mature enough to survive without the massage of the contractions and birth canal passage, which helps release the lipoprotein substance that bathes the baby's lungs like a lubricant and helps them expand and contract.

Marshall Klaus[12] and John Kennell,[13] both world-renowned pediatricians, have coined several terms for the new birthing practices they started, including "lying-in" or "rooming-in," one of the first mother/baby staying-together arrangements in obstetric hospitals, and "bonding," which loosely means "being glued" to someone. They even appropriated words from other languages, including *doula*, the Greek word for a woman who helps the mother, as well as the father, through labor.

According to Marshall Klaus,[12] the doula touches the mother, holds the mother, and explains what is happening during labor. She praises the mother, tries to be supportive, and tries to coach the mother at the mother's own pace. As Dr. Klaus reported in our book *Touch During Early Development*,[14] the mothers who had a doula during labor and delivery stroked their babies more, and they smiled at and talked to their babies longer during their infants' first hour of life. The mothers who had a doula rated their babies and husbands more favorably, and they also breastfed for a longer period of time.

According to Dr. Kennell, the custom in 127 out of 128 non-industrial societies is to have another woman present during labor.[13] According to the data in this study, having a doula results in fewer perinatal complications, less delivery medication, lower rates of cesarean section, shorter labor, and fewer infants being admitted to the neonatal intensive care units.[14] Over half the time, the doulas were observed touching the mother, using various touching methods: rubbing and stroking her head, holding her extremities, rubbing and stroking her trunk in early labor, and holding her trunk in later labor, particularly during contractions.

Throughout evolution and across cultures, the laboring woman has received significant amounts of touching from those assisting her with labor, usually other women. But for American obstetrics, this procedure is new and is rarely used, probably because insurance companies do not cover the doula—a shortsighted measure on their part, given that they could be saving many thousands of dollars in reduced perinatal complications and improved neonatal outcome. Certainly the costs of cesarean sections and treating premature newborns, along with the associated hospital bed costs, far outweigh the costs of doulas and massage therapists, but their myopic answer to this would no doubt be that their way is "proven," doulas are not.

To help reduce labor complications, we conducted a study on massage therapy during labor.[15] Twenty-eight women were recruited from prenatal classes and randomly assigned to receive massages, as well as coaching in breathing from their partners during labor, or to receive coaching in breathing alone (a technique learned during prenatal classes). The massaged mothers reported they were less depressed and had less anxiety and pain, and they showed less agitated activity and anxiety after the first massage during labor. In addition, the massaged mothers had significantly shorter labors, a shorter hospital stay, and less postpartum depression.

Postpartum complications such as muscle spasms, congestion, and postpartum depression can also be prevented by massage therapy. In Malaysia, mothers are routinely massaged by their mother or grandmother on the second day after giving birth, and then every day for six weeks after that. Massaging dilates the mothers' blood vessels, which generally improves their overall circulation and helps prevent muscle spasms and congestion. In one of our studies, we gave depressed teenage mothers thirty-minute massages twice a week for a month after they had given birth; these massages not only alleviated their depression and their stress hormone levels (decreased cortisol), but also increased their serotonin levels.[16] The serotonin increase may also have helped to decrease their depression, inasmuch as serotonin is the body's natural equivalent of the chemical used in such antidepressants as Prozac. Another positive effect of the massaging was that EEG waves shifted from the right side of the brain, which processes negative emotions, to the left side, which processes positive emotions.[17] We then had these depressed teenage mothers massage their infants, which not only helped the infants but also helped the mothers in their relationship with their infants.

Almost all nonindustrial societies (183 of 186) expect mothers and babies to stay together for days or weeks after delivery. Virtually nobody allows the kinds of separations that are routine in many hospitals in the United States. According to John Kennell, mothers who receive caressing and holding by doulas or significant others during delivery begin to explore their infants immediately after delivery, starting their exploration by touching the infant's limbs with their fingertips, and proceeding within minutes to massaging the trunk with their palms.[18]

In another study, Doctors Klaus and Kennell had mothers handle their nude infants for an hour during the first two hours after birth and for five extra hours during the next three days.[19] At an interview one month after birth, they found that, compared to the mothers with only routine contact, the mothers who had handled their infants for the extra hours soothed their infants more, fondled and made eye contact more often during feedings, spent more time assisting the doctor during the one-year examinations, asked more questions and gave fewer commands to their children two years later, and had children who scored higher on IQ and language tests at five years. Interestingly, John Kennell found that the best predictor of the amount of time a young mother spent with her newborn infant was the amount of time that she herself had spent in contact with her own mother as an infant.[20]

Given the considerable amount of contact, it is perhaps not surprising that mothers can recognize their infants by touch soon after birth. In a study by Marsha Kaitz and her colleagues from Hebrew University in Jerusalem, women who held their infants for at least one hour after delivery were able to identify their own babies when they were blindfolded and placed in front of a row of newborns[21] by just touching their hands and their foreheads. Fathers could also identify their own newborns, but only by their hands.[22] Parenthetically, Kaitz and her colleagues also found that blindfolded lovers could identify each other merely by touching their lover's hand.[23]

Touch is critical for the infant's bonding. During the newborn period, most of an infant's affections are tactile.[24] The infant affectionately pats the breast while nursing, and months later pats the mother's face and shares kisses. Although the period around birth is considered the most important for bonding between parent and child, the bonding actually begins before the birth, particularly now that parents can view ultrasound pictures of their baby and listen to its heartbeat. Some parents even read to their babies on a daily basis and stimulate them with vibrators, as mentioned earlier.

We conducted a study providing pregnant women with ultrasound feedback.[25] They were shown the video of their child during the ultrasound, and the ultrasonographer described the baby's body parts and movements. As we had hoped, this procedure reduced prenatal anxiety, but we were surprised to also find that the mothers also became more attached to their babies. Another surprise was that these newborns weighed more, were less fussy, and were more responsive to their parents compared to newborns whose mothers did not receive ultrasound feedback. By reducing the mother's anxiety levels, there were probably fewer stress hormones crossing the placenta that could cause the baby to have growth delays and could possibly lead to a hypersensitive nervous system. Changes for the better in the mothers' habits (improved eating and sleeping, for example) that were due to lowered stress levels could also explain why the newborns weighed more and were less irritable than babies born to mothers with higher stress levels.

We also learned that we could predict postpartum depression by asking, "Do you and your partner want this baby?" From our own research, we now know that postpartum depression, affecting as much as 80 percent of women, has terrible effects on newborns.[26] Babies born to depressed mothers show inferior performance on the Brazelton Neonatal Behavior Assessment, an examination that assesses the newborn's response to visual, auditory, social, and nonsocial stimulation, and the newborn's motor behavior, self-quieting, and reflexes.[26] These newborns are also less attentive and less responsive to faces,[27] and their perception of auditory, tactile, and visual stimuli is less developed.[28] In addition, their EEG activity is similar to that of their adult mothers.[29] The differences at this early stage probably derive from these babies having been exposed to their mother's high levels of stress hormones during pregnancy,[32] because at birth the newborns have the same high stress-hormone levels as their mothers.[30] After their birth, the depressed mothers touched their newborns less often than the nondepressed mothers.[31] When a mother's depression continues, the infant's growth and development are delayed. If the mother is still depressed six months after the delivery, the infant typically weighs less than the norm, and at one year has lower Bayley mental and motor scale scores.

Doctors Klaus and Kennell have long believed that when a mother is separated from her infant during the newborn period, she feels helpless and depressed.[19] They argue that she needs to be an active participant in the baby's care, not only for the baby's well-being, but for her own as well, and they started the lying-in practice just so mothers could be the ones primarily responsible for the continuous care of their newborns. They also advocated early contact, with infants being placed skin-to-skin on their mother's chest immediately after birth (figure 3.2), a practice that inspired dozens of studies around the world. Overall, the resulting studies suggest that those mothers who have early contact are more satisfied with their infants, spend more time looking at their infants' faces, and more time interacting with them. The early contact infants also cry less and smile at their mothers more than the separated infants.

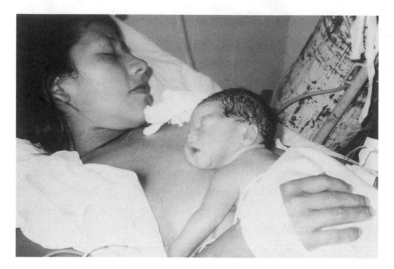

Figure 3.2
Mother and infant in skin-to-skin contact. Courtesy of Gene Cranston Anderson, PhD, RN, FAAN.

Early Separation

Dr. Myron Hofer has studied the effects of maternal separation on mother rats and their rat pups as a model of extreme separation.[33] Hofer noted that the separation experience led to a state of increased excitability for the rat pups who, ultimately, died. In utero, a fetus receives continuous tactile stimulation and feedback from the mother's heart rate, respiration rate, and other physiological rhythms; then suddenly, after birth, it is in the outside world without all that. At this crucial time, the rat pup needs its mother's thermal and tactile stimulation to prevent it from becoming hyperexcitable. Even though Hofer tried to create substitute mother rats by covering a heater with a fur pelt, he was unable to return the rat pups to a normal state with this fake mother.

Prematurity

Babies who are born prematurely are separated from their mother for long periods of time. Premature infants are touch-deprived because, to keep them alive, they are placed in incubators for the first several days. Dr. Allen Gottfried observed that those infants receive mostly nonsocial touching in the incubator.[34] Unfortunately, the premature nursery has traditionally been the no-touch center of the hospital. As one sensitive neonatal nurse has suggested, "the incubator is an impregnable fortress on no-parent land, protected from assault from touch-crazed mothers and fathers by the glass curtain." Not surprisingly, then, mothers of premature babies take much longer to progress from fingertip touch to holding in a body caress, probably because these mothers view their preterm infants as fragile.

Many neonatal intensive care nurseries have minimal-touch, or no-touch signs because of a concern that any stimulation could cause physiological disorganization in sick, premature infants. This practice evolved because invasive touch such as drawing blood and inserting life-sustaining feeding tubes led to undesirable effects such as apnea (breathing cessation) and bradycardia (heart rate slowing). Unfortunately for the premature babies, all kinds of touch got lumped into the negative category, including gentle touch, even though that kind of touch has been shown to have positive effects. In our studies, for example, we noted that babies given a nipple to suck on cried less during blood-drawing procedures (figure 3.3), probably because sucking and crying are incompatible.[35] Similarly, when we stroked infants, they became quiet and alert rather than aroused and physiologically disorganized.[36]

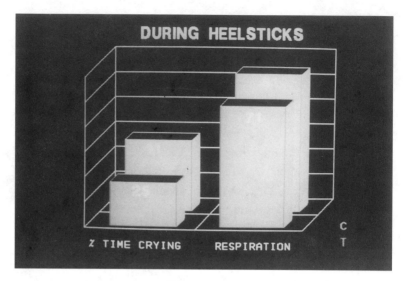

Figure 3.3
Decreased crying during nonnutrive sucking.

Increasing Tactile Stimulation

Dozens of studies have shown the positive effects that different kinds of touching have on premature babies, including stroking, rocking, waterbeds, and breathing bears. For example, researcher M. Neal found that infants who were rocked gained more weight and were better able to track visual and auditory stimuli than nonrocked infants.[37] D. Freedman and his colleagues showed that the rocked twin of twin pairs gained more weight.[38] In separate studies, P. B. Rausch[39] and J. White and R. LaBarba[40] found that moving the infant's limbs led to greater weight gain, and greater activity and alertness in the infants.

Other forms of tactile stimulation such as waterbeds are helpful. Dr. Anneliese Korner and her collaborators at Stanford

University Medical Center learned that waterbeds in incubators could reduce apnea in premature infants.[41] Her colleague, Dr. Evelyn Thoman, developed the breathing bear, a blue bear whose audible breathing rhythm was synchronized with the baby's natural breathing rhythm and then placed in the infant's incubator. The infants who had this breathing bear gradually moved to its corner of the crib to be in touch with it, and because of the bear's similar breathing rhythm, the infants' breathing became more organized.[42] This is reminiscent of Dr. Hofer's study on rat mothers and his conclusion that the mother's rhythm organizes the baby's breathing.[33] Rocking and bear's breathing approximate the mother's respiratory rate, and the mother's patting and stroking movements may approximate her heart rate. When the infant is separated from the mother, it uses its own rhythmic patterns, such as body-rocking and sucking on thumbs and/or pacifiers, to help organize its activity. These rhythmic behaviors continue throughout infancy.

Mothers must have intuitively sensed the importance of rhythmical stimulation even before the breathing and heartbeat bears appeared on the market. In a study by Dr. Lee Salk, mothers showed a preference for holding their infant on the left side, which Salk speculated was because of the baby's need to continue hearing the mother's heartbeat.[43] (Others suggested this was the preferred position because it freed the mother's right hand.) In the Salk group, infants held on the left side gained more weight, cried less, had fewer respiratory and gastrointestinal difficulties, and had deeper, more regular breathing.

Infants also receive a lot of stimulation by mouth. From the first moments of life, the mouth has a sophisticated role to play—not surprising because, next to the hand, the mouth involves the largest part of the sensory and motor cortex in the brain. Sucking, and knowing how to suck differently on the breast, the bottle, or the pacifier, requires considerable skill. These activities are, in fact, so complex that they are considered wired-in at a very early stage in prenatal development. Some babies are such avid suckers in the womb that they are born with abrasions on their hands. Premature newborns, even when they are tube fed, will gain more weight if they suck on a pacifier during their tube feedings.[44]

Sucking on pacifiers is good, not bad, for babies. In one of our nurseries, newborns need a prescription for a pacifier because someone was worried about cross-contamination from accidentally sharing pacifiers. As a result, there is bedlam in that nursery with all the crying babies. Crying is very disorganizing and energy-consuming for the infant and, of course, very annoying for the caregiver. Excessive crying at the six-week to six-month period (also called colic) is probably the worst problem and the worst stage in a baby's development. Unfortunately, the cause of colic is not yet known and nothing seems to work. We are currently trying massage therapy for colicky babies because infant massage therapists claim that it works beautifully. Fortunately, like a developmental milestone, colic disappears by six months. But the fussing that continues across early development for most children can be significantly reduced by pacifiers. I think it would be a good idea for infants to have an assortment of toylike pacifiers of all sizes, shapes, and textures, for early exploring by mouth, and for keeping children calmed down.

Another sophisticated mouth behavior that may be wired-in is imitation. Within the first few hours after birth, newborns can imitate happy, sad, and surprised facial expressions simply by feeling the way their mouth is moving as they watch a person's face and try to move their mouths as the person does

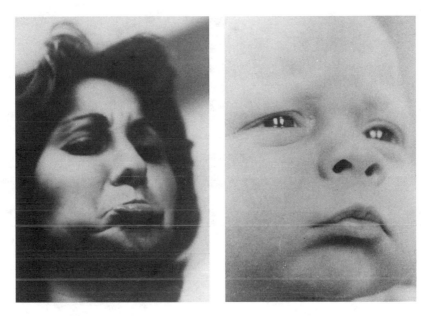

Figure 3.4
Newborn imitating facial expressions.

(figure 3.4).[45] But not all newborns do this; some are more poker-faced than others.

Carrying

Another form of touch that also comforts and soothes infants, particularly preterm infants, is kangaroo care. Originating in Bogota, Colombia, this is another early-touch practice, so named because it resembles the way that marsupials care for their young. In this kind of care, the mother or father holds the diaper-clad or naked infant beneath his or her clothing, skin-to-skin, and the infant lies between the mother's breasts, or on the father's chest (figure 3.5). In this position, the infants

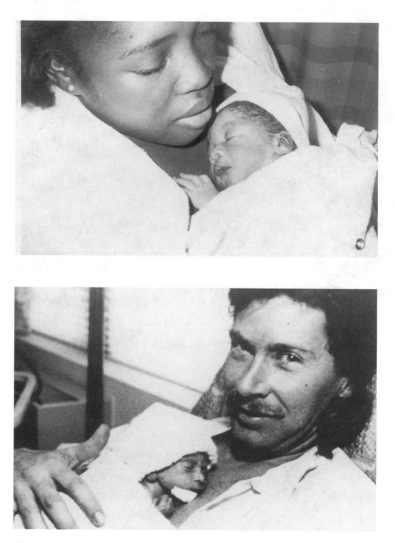

Figure 3.5
Parents holding their infant in "kangaroo care" fashion.

are warm, and they have regular heart rates and respiration, and adequate oxygenation. They also sleep more deeply, have more alert inactivity, and cry less. In addition, mothers who practice kangaroo care breastfeed and become more attached to their infants. According to Gene Anderson, a nurse-researcher who has conducted many of these studies, kangaroo care also promotes normal growth of the head because the upright position of the baby's head means it is not being pushed into the mattress.[46] Although kangaroo care is becoming increasingly popular in neonatal intensive care units here, it is used even more in countries outside the United States.

The Kalahari San hunter-gatherers carry their infants over 90 percent of the daylight hours, but in the United States, holding and carrying infants occurs for only two to three hours a day in the first few months of life, and even less for older infants. A study by Ron Barr from McGill University in Canada showed that additional time spent carrying by mothers resulted in less crying by infants, particularly at the peak crying time (six weeks of age).[47] This difference amounted to 43 percent less crying over a twenty-four hour period. In addition, the peak crying at six weeks disappeared.

Touch during Early Interactions

Among the Efe hunter-gatherer tribes in Africa, the mothers touch and hold their babies about 50 percent of the time. According to Ed Tronick and his colleagues who studied these tribes, the father's contact was significantly less than the mother's, and the mother's rate of contact decreased over the first few years.[48] In other studies, these researchers found that, in the United States, mothers spend about 60 percent of their interaction time touching their infants, with the largest portion of that time spent rhythmically stroking and holding the infant.

Tickling and kissing occur less often and more discretely, but by the age of two, these infants have learned to hug and kiss. The same studies done on depressed mothers, however, showed that the mothers poked and jabbed the infants more frequently, which caused the infants to fuss and turn away.[48]

Touch in Childhood and Adolescence

Ashley Montagu tells the story that "In 1894, Luther Emmett Holt, Professor of Pediatrics at Cornell University Medical School, published a booklet entitled *The Care and Feeding of Children*.[49] In its fifteenth edition, in 1935, Holt recommended bottlefeeding (just as good as breastfeeding, he claimed), the abolition of the cradle, that one should not pick up a child, no matter how long it cries, and that it should be fed only at four-hour intervals." About the same time, Professor John Watson also wrote a book in which he said, "There is a sensible way of treating children. Never hug and kiss them, never let them sit in your lap. If you must, kiss them once on the forehead when they say good night and shake hands with them in the morning."[49] Sadly, most of our culture has heeded that advice throughout much of the twentieth century.

The soothing stimulation by the parents and the self-stimulation rhythms of the infant are quickly replaced by peer play (rough and tumble play at the preschool stage, and contact sports through grade school and high school). As children grow older, physical contact becomes more taboo, at least from parent or adult to child.

By the time children reach junior high, they are receiving about half the touch they did in the primary grades, and the touching is different—more shoulder to shoulder, elbow to elbow, rather than hand contact. In adolescence, the touching may pick up if there are intimate relationships. The adolescent typically treats family members as if they had some terrible disease. Given touch taboos, it is not surprising that touch-deprived adolescents (and some adults) might be drawn to touch-dancing, skinny-dipping, nude beaches, and waterbeds. Other adolescent touch institutions include extremely long showers, marathon sunbathing, applying lots of makeup, and peer backrubs in ninth-grade classrooms, which seem to have evolved around the same time the schools mandated that teachers could no longer hug or touch children. Unisex backrubs and hugging seem to be as commonplace in high school settings now as the former boyfriend/girlfriend necking and petting from an earlier time (figure 3.6).

Touch in Adulthood

In *Touching*, Ashley Montagu says,

The French wit who defined sexual intercourse as "the harmony of two souls and the contact of two epidermis," elegantly emphasized a basic truth—the massive involvement of the skin and sexual congress. The truth is that in no other relationship is the skin so totally involved as in sexual intercourse. Sex, indeed, has been called the highest form of touch. In the profoundest sense, touch is the true language of sex. The lips and the external genitalia are especially well-supplied with concave, disk-like branched sensory nerve endings.[50]

Montagu forgot to mention that the lips and genitalia are also extremely well-endowed with sebaceous glands, which secrete sebum, a moisturizer-type substance that is thought to behave like a pheromone. Pheromones are usually odors, like musk, that attract individuals to each other, but in this case the pheromone-like sebum involves taste and may facilitate kissing, attachments, and sexual intimacy.

The functional significance of kissing is unknown. Desmond Morris suggests that

Figure 3.6
Young children loving touching.

In early human societies, before commercial baby food was invented, mothers weaned their children by chewing up their food and then passing it into the infantile mouth by a lip-to-lip contact—which naturally involved a lot of tonguing and intramouth pressure. A form of bird-like system of parental care seems strange and alien to us today, but our species probably practiced it for a million years or more, and adult erotic kissing today is almost certainly a relic gesture stemming from these origins.[51]

Another possibility is that kissing occurs because the lips are particularly well-endowed with sebaceous glands, and the sebum might facilitate attachment between mother and baby and between lovers.

For some, the most meaningful part of sexual intimacy is simply close contact. In a survey of 100,000 people reported by Ann Landers, the question was asked, "Would you be content to be held close and treated tenderly and forget about the sex act?"[52] Seventy-two percent of the respondents said yes—and 40 percent of those answering yes were under forty years of age. Some have noted that body contact, particularly for a woman, is a very intimate act. At all ages, beginning from birth, women have lower touch and pain thresholds than men, which may explain why women are more responsive to touching than men. However, boys are handled less, caressed less often, and held for shorter periods than girls, which could explain why they are less responsive to touch. At a later age, though, according to the *Hite Report on Male Sexuality*, men catch up to women and also desire more non-sex-related touching from women.

In the Sensate Focus System of sex therapy designed by Masters and Johnson, no intercourse is allowed for the first few weeks of sex therapy.[53] Couples simply practice touching each other's body instead. This takes away some of the performance anxiety and enhances the desire for sex.

Some go so far as to say touch is our strongest contact. In the words of our colleague Saul Schanberg,

Touch is ten times stronger than verbal or emotional contact, and it affects damned near everything we do. No other sense can arouse you like touch. We always knew that, but we never realized it had a biological basis. If touch did not feel good, there would be no species, parenthood, or survival. The mother would not touch her baby in the right way unless the mother felt pleasure in doing it. If we did not like the feel of touching and patting one another, we would not have had sex. Those animals that did more touching instinctively produced offspring which survived and had more energy, and so passed around their tendency to touch which became even stronger. We forget that *touch is not only basic to our species, but the key to it.*[54]

4

Touch Deprivation

The Stigma of Touch

At least 30 percent of girls and 10 percent of boys are sexually molested before they are eighteen years old.[1] This high incidence of sexual abuse has unfortunately been a great deterrent to healthy sexual development. Parents and teachers have become afraid to touch children because their physical affection might be misinterpreted, so children are deprived of touch at a very early age. This fear is also the reason many daycare centers no longer employ male teachers; the loss of their potential as role models is another way the stigma of touch leads to touch deprivation.

In the words of Ashley Montagu, "Such alarm is understandable in a society that has so confounded love, sex, affection, and touch. The genuinely loving parents have nothing to fear from their demonstrative acts of affection for the children or anyone else."[2] The problem with the confusion over affection toward children is that it has made parents and teachers paranoid about hugging and touching children, and children have had to tolerate significantly less affection.

In a recent National Public Radio interview, the director of a model preschool in Massachusetts said that her teachers are not allowed to touch the children because of potential lawsuits.

Asked by a caller what her teachers would do if a child was hurt on the playground and came running to one of them, she answered in a rather dispassionate tone that her teachers would be advised not to touch or hold the child.

We recently conducted a study at the Touch Research Institute Nursery School to observe three aspects of touch: the different types of touching the children received from their teachers and from the other children; where on the body the touch occurred; and whether the touch seemed to be for communication purposes or for affection.[3] We found that, despite our being a model nursery school, the teachers touched the children very little, particularly as the children grew older (figure 4.1). When we showed the data to the teachers, they said they touched very little because of a concern that their touching might be misconstrued as sexual abuse. After a discussion on the acceptable types and places for touch, the teachers

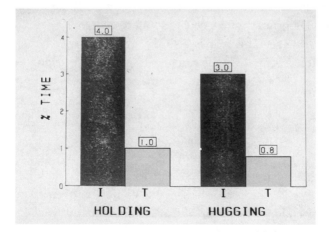

Figure 4.1
Percent observation time holding and hugging observed in preschool nursery. (I, infant; T, toddler)

increased their touching, particularly their affectionate touching.

The stigma of touch extends to adolescents and adults, as a study at Swarthmore College suggests, in which students were told they were going to be taken to a darkened room of people and then to a lighted room of people.[4] In the dark room, more than 90 percent of the student strangers touched each other, and almost 50 percent of them hugged each other, whereas almost none of the subjects in the lighted room did so. The students were too shy to touch each other when they could be seen, but were more willing to touch in the anonymous dark. In another experiment, students confined to a completely dark room for one week experienced a marked increase in touch sensitivity, as well as sensitivity to pain.

In most psychiatric units for young people across the world, there is a "no-touch" policy derived from staff concern about potential sexual-abuse accusations and about promiscuity between the adolescents. To counter this, we recently conducted a massage-therapy study on one of these units to introduce touch to adolescent psychiatric patients.[5] After being massaged one-half hour a day for a week, these adolescents were less depressed and less anxious than they had been, and their stress hormones (cortisol and norepinephrine) had decreased. They also developed better organized sleep patterns and showed more appropriate behavior after massage therapy. Despite these significant changes, which led to the adolescents being discharged earlier, with resulting savings in hospital costs, the program was never adopted. When the staff was asked what happened, they expressed two concerns, one of them being the sex of the therapist. If the therapist was of the opposite sex, they felt some sexual acting out might occur. If the therapist was the same sex, there was concern that the adolescents might become homophobic. Although neither problem was reflected in our data, we switched to using volunteer grandparents as massage therapists to allay staff fears. The staff's second concern was that the patients talked more during massage therapy than during psychotherapy. They therefore wanted us to tape-record the sessions for their use. Because we felt this could negatively affect the massage therapy, our solution was to tell the young people that massages are better without talking (which they usually are). With these adjustments, the program continued successfully.

In the 1960s, American adolescents and adults made a special effort to overcome the by-then-recognized stigma against touching by joining sensitivity training, encounter, and marathon groups. This "human potential" movement was oriented toward touch. Touch activities included backrubs, massages, hands-on relaxation exercises, trust exercises (one person falls back into the arms of the other), love baths (everyone in the group hugs one another), and blind walks (one person leads a blindfolded partner on a walking journey, teaching that person tactile discrimination). The movement inspired a number of books on touch, including Jane Howard's *Please Touch*,[6] and a novel by Glenn Davis, called *Touching*.[7] Doctors Carl Rogers[8] and J. R. Gibb[9] reviewed dozens of studies on these groups. They both concluded that the groups helped reduce the stigma against touching. In spite of this, however, America still remains a touch-taboo culture.

Other Side Effects of Touch Deprivation

Physical Violence

Several investigators, including Dr. J. H. Prescott, have suggested that touch deprivation in childhood leads to physical violence.[10] He has reported that most juvenile delinquents and criminals come from neglectful or abusive parents, and he believes that "the deprivation of body touch, contact and movement are the basic causes of a number of emotional disturbances including depressive and autistic behaviors, hyperactivity, sexual aberration, drug abuse, violence and aggression."[10] His theory is that the lack of sensory stimulation in childhood leads to an addiction to sensory stimulation in adulthood, resulting in delinquency, drug use, and crime. This theory came from a study conducted in forty-nine non-industrial cultures, from the Ainu in Japan to the Zuni in New Mexico. All these cultures were notably similar, except that high rates of adult violence were observed in those cultures where the children received very little physical affection, and no adult violence occurred in those cultures with high levels of physical affection toward children. These findings could, of course, relate to other things, such as parental sexual abuse, although the study found no cultural differences on this or any other variables.

Sleep Disturbance
Touch deprivation is also harmful to children because it severely affects their sleep. Sleep is necessary as a stress reducer and for conservation of energy. The researchers Heinicke and Westheimer studied two-year-old children who were separated from their parents for two to twenty weeks and living in an institution where they received less touch.[11] Even after the children were reunited with their parents, most of them continued to have sleep disturbances, including difficulty in falling asleep or remaining asleep. In all our studies where very young children were separated from their mothers, whether it was because their mothers were hospitalized for the birth of another child or because their mothers were away at out-of-town conferences, the children's sleep was always affected.[12] They took

longer to fall asleep and they awoke more frequently during the night. Although these children sometimes continued their "normal classroom behavior," their sleep (both naptime and nighttime sleep) was the most affected of all the behaviors observed (figure 4.2).

Suppressed Immune Response
Touch deprivation also affects the immune system. Steve Suomi has conducted a number of immune studies with monkeys, testing the relationship between physical contact and the body's ability to respond to an immunological challenge (a tetanus shot).[13] He found a direct relationship between the amount of contact and the amount of grooming an infant received in the first six or seven months of life and its ability to produce antibodies in response to an antibody challenge at a little over a year of age. In several studies following separation of monkeys from their mothers, Suomi and his colleagues found suppressed immune response,[13] including less natural killer cell activity (natural killer cells are the front line of the immune system and are noted for warding off viral and cancer cells).

One way that touch might influence the immune system is by lowering arousal levels and their accompanying stress hormones that dampen the immune system. Social grooming among pigtail monkeys, for example, is associated with a decrease in heart rate and stress hormones.[13] In turn, the monkeys' immune function improves. (It also improves in people who receive deep-pressure touch.[14])

A compromised immune system can also result from sleep disturbances, which, as discussed, can be caused by touch deprivation. Dr. Martin Reite and his colleagues at the University of Colorado Medical Center found that after a two-week separation from their mothers, infant bonnet monkeys

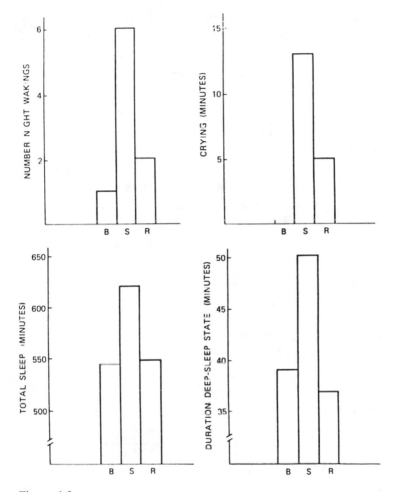

Figure 4.2
Percent time sleep behaviors occurred during maternal separation. (B, baseline; S, separation; R, reunion)

experienced both sleep disturbances and a suppressed immune system,[16] but the latter returned to normal after the infant monkeys were reunited with their mothers. The monkeys who were separated from their mothers also showed depressed behavior, including huddling in corners and changes in body temperature, heart rate, brain waves, and sleep patterns; some of these symptoms persisted even after they were reunited with their mothers.

In our studies on touch deprivation among preschool children who were separated from their mothers, we noted more frequent illnesses, particularly constipation, diarrhea, and upper respiratory infections.[12] In another study on ten-week-old infants, when the mothers were taught to massage their infants' backs, giving them extra tactile stimulation,[15] the opposite effects were noted: these infants experienced fewer colds and less diarrhea approximately four months later.

The skin secretes an immune hormone similar to the hormone from the thymus gland that produces T cells. T cells are a significant part of the immune system because they destroy antigens and are important for those who have cancer or similar diseases. Ironically, both the immune system and the skin immune hormone are compromised because these diseases tend to decrease the desire for sex (even though people with cancer may desire more physical closeness), which keeps the skin hormone from being secreted. Just when the immune systems of these people are severely compromised, their immune problem seems to be compounded by their lack of interest in sexual intimacy; but there are other forms of intimacy, including holding, backrubbing, and comforting touch, which could compensate.

Growth Deprivation

Touch deprivation also delays growth. Dr. Saul Schanberg of Duke University Medical School has conducted many animal studies on this. Most of Dr. Schanberg's research has been conducted with mother rats and their pups. Rats happen to be very good analogical subjects for growth in humans because both rats and people have similar responses to deprivation and stimulation. Dr. Schanberg noticed that when rat pups are deprived of their mothers, they experience a significant decline in growth hormone and ornithine decarboxylase (ODC), which is part of the protein synthesis chain and important for proper functioning of the immune system.[17] Decreases in ODC, resulting in a weakened immune system, are noted in the brain, heart, liver, and virtually every organ of the body following separation, but returning the rat pups to their mothers reverses the decline.

Dr. Schanberg noticed these declines but could not figure out what was causing them. He and his colleagues knew the answer was related to something the mother rat was doing to the pups, but they did not know what that was until, during Dr. Schanberg's absence to attend a conference, one of his graduate students sat observing the mother rat and her pups day and night and was able to figure out exactly what the mother was doing to the pups. He raced out of the lab with a "Eureka" scream, and came back with a little paint brush in his hand. He proceeded to dip this paint brush into water and "lick" the pups deprived of their mothers by stroking his brush on them in a regular, even rhythm, to reverse the effects of maternal deprivation. When Dr. Schanberg and his students later tried mimicking what they observed mother rats doing (carrying the pups around, tail-pinching, and tongue-licking), only the tongue-licking returned the deprived rat pups to a normal state.

Dr. Schanberg noted that when he first published some of this work he got numerous letters from people who told him that their mothers had touched them a lot during their early development, but in spite of this, they were not chosen to play center on the basketball team because they were only 5'8". Dr. Schanberg could only answer that genes are, of course, the primary determinants of height, but stimulation is what helps to get those genes expressed.

Recently, Dr. Schanberg located a growth gene that is responsible for this touch stimulation/growth relationship.[17] He and his collaborators ran an experiment preparing some RNA from the livers of deprived and nondeprived pups, and with the use of a specific probe that could identify CFOS (a messenger gene), they found that maternal deprivation significantly reduced this messenger. This is interesting because molecular biologists had sworn that environmental factors such as touch could not affect genes. As Dr. Schanberg said, "In terms of what we might be looking at in the future, I believe the brain (reacting to the environment) can stick its long arm down right into the middle of a cell and regulate a gene, which is the basic unit of life itself. In that regard we have to give some credit to Michelangelo, who some several hundred years ago said, 'to touch can be to give life'. I do not think he meant it exactly the same way, but I think he is right."[17]

Growth deprivation was first labeled "psychosocial dwarfism" by Doctors Powell, Brasel, and Blizzard at Johns Hopkins University Medical School.[18] In their 1967 report, they noted growth deprivation, endocrine deficits, and speech and behavior problems, a set of conditions now commonly called "failure to thrive." Back in 1951, Dr. Widdowson of Cambridge University first reported the different effects of good and bad orphanages on this growth deprivation syndrome.[19] The children in orphanages run by caring caregivers thrived, but those in lesser environments did not do well. World War II elicited many anecdotal reports by famous people in the field, including René Spitz, John Bowlby, Anna Freud, and Dorothy Burlingham, which led to positive reforms in this area, the obvious exceptions being the orphanages in Romania where recent exposés suggest that those children were so touch-starved that they failed to grow to half their expected height or weight and also, as recent studies suggest, failed to develop normal cognitive and motor skills.

In our volume, *Touch in Early Development*, Montagu refers to the origins of stunted growth:

For many years I longed to give a lecture entitled, "Radiology and Love." I *have* given that lecture, but no medical school would permit me to use that title because my kind sponsor said, "No one will understand what on earth you are talking about from that title." What does radiology have to do with love? If a person has been unloved during childhood, you will see lines of retarded growth in the tibia or shinbone of that individual. You will (also) see it in the x-ray of the hand bones of a newborn baby, if the mother has had an emotionally disturbing pregnancy.[20]

Depleted growth hormone may also be a factor in delayed bone growth, although this is less clear in people than in the deprived rat pups.

Throughout the nineteenth and early twentieth centuries, children raised in orphanages had a less than fifty-fifty chance of reaching puberty. At the turn of the century, the German Foundling Home had a mortality rate of over 70 percent for infants. In the early 1900s, American orphanages had infant death rates that averaged 32–75 percent. Even worse, Baltimore institutions were estimated to have at least a 90 percent mortality rate, and it was closer to 100 percent at New York's Randall Island Hospital.[21]

In 1945, researcher R. Spitz compared two children's orphanages,[22] a prison nursery for convicted women and infants, and a foundling home. Both provided well-prepared food, adequate clothing, and good medical services, and both were clean and well staffed, although the foundling home children were significantly better off in that respect. Despite the better hygiene for the foundling-home children, however, they fared worse (including a higher mortality rate during a measles epidemic) and experienced motor and mental deterioration, in contrast to the nursery children, who had the convicted women as mother substitutes, and who, according to Spitz's study, excelled in both motor and cognitive development.

Children with failure-to-thrive syndrome have diminished growth hormone, although, after only one day recuperating in the hospital, their growth hormone response is able to recover. Some say the rat studies suggest that physical contact stimulates growth hormone, but this relationship of stimulation to growth hormone is less understood in humans. In the 1970s, Wayne Dennis researched the legalization of adoption in Lebanon and noted IQs in the 50s in the orphanage children.[23] After the children were placed in nurturing homes, their IQs rose to normal levels, the only exceptions being those children who had been in the orphanage for more than two years. With these children, adoption did not make up for the loss in intelligence.

Given all that we know about touch deprivation in these tragic "experiments in nature," it is somewhat surprising that we still hospitalize children in "germ-free" bubbles where they are deprived of human touch. Reports by Dr. Holland and her colleagues at the University of Buffalo School of Medicine and Dr. Hollenbach at the American Association of Retired Persons suggested that there were too many negative changes in behavior, sleep patterns, and physiology following isolation in these bubbles,[24] leaving open the question of how much the progression of diseases like cancer is related to the touch-deprivation effects on the immune system.

In Montagu's book, an adult patient who was placed in a bubble described his experience:

About a week ago, it started to get on my nerves . . . not being able to feel other people and hoping I could soon come out. I felt like everything was closing in on me and I couldn't stand it anymore. I just had *to feel* other people, I wanted to feel somebody, touch another human being. If I could have done this, I could have stuck it out longer . . . but I couldn't, there was no way I could touch anyone or in any way express my feelings toward somebody just by touching their hand or squeezing it. This is very difficult to explain—it leaves you at a loss for words. You just feel you are all alone in the world and everything is cold. There is no warmth. The warmth is all gone, and you just feel like there isn't anything.[25]

A child's words would be less articulate, but the slumped, depressed posture that is typical of children encased in bubbles speaks volumes.[26]

Tactile Sensitivity and Allergic Conditions

Some children seem to be born with an aversion to touch that can result in touch deprivation by their own doing. Some of these aversions could result from a genetic predisposition; others appear to be learned, conditioned responses. For example, many preterm babies who receive invasive procedures, primarily in the chest and abdomen region, develop extremely averse reactions to being touched in that region, as we discovered when we conducted our studies on them—they would not let us massage those areas.

Autism
Children with autism are thought to be innately averse to touch. Even though most people describe these children as

being resistant to cuddling, we are finding, to the contrary, that they respond to touch with pressure and enjoy being massaged (see massage therapy, chapter 7). Dr. Older, for example, described a class of children with Down's syndrome as being encouraged to hug children with autism and how the children with autism were very responsive to being hugged by children their same size.[26] Dr. Waal has also reported that certain kinds of touch (massaging and hugging) seem to be accepted by these children,[27] possibly because these forms of touch are less arousing. In the chapter on massage therapy with children, we describe two studies we conducted using massage therapy on children with autism, with the massage given by either the parent[28] or a therapist.[29] In both studies, the children loved being massaged.

Dermatitis and Asthma

In the case of autism, touch deprivation is blamed on the disorder: the child refuses touch and thereby causes his own deprivation. In other disorders, it's the reverse: the touch deprivation itself is thought to be responsible for the disorder. For example, several researchers have attributed allergies such as dermatitis and asthma to touch deprivation. In a study by Dr. Maurice Rosenthal, the majority of a group of children with eczema had mothers who failed to touch them sufficiently.[30] Although the reason is unclear, this immune problem may relate to the fact that the skin and the thymus need stimulation in order to produce their immune cells. Parents are often advised to apply medication (as in a massage) to provide additional tactile stimulation. In *Touching Is Healing*, Jules Older says he believes that a study comparing self-applied to spouse-applied medications for skin conditions such as psoriasis would show that having someone else apply the medication is far more effective.[32]

Asthma, often associated with dermatitis, is another chronic disease that often starts in childhood and is usually related to allergic reactions. This allergy has also been anecdotally traced to touch deprivation. Ashley Montagu reports a case of twin sisters who suffered frequent asthma attacks.[32] They had lost their mother at birth and, as a result, had experienced very minimal touch stimulation. Dr. Montagu prescribed massage therapy for one of the twins he happened to visit; that twin's asthma attacks stopped after receiving the massage therapy. The other twin's asthma attacks improved following her marriage, but after getting a divorce, she died of an asthma attack.

At the Touch Research Institutes, we have conducted studies using massage therapy with children who have asthma[33] and atopic dermatitis[34] (see chapter 7). After receiving massage therapy from their parents for a month, the children with asthma had fewer asthma attacks and showed improved pulmonary function; the children with atopic dermatitis had less eczema.

Cardiovascular Disease

Cardiovascular disease is often exacerbated by a lack of contact with other people, whereas those who have more contact with others seem to be protected from the disease. As Jules Older suggests, heart disease prevention has focused on smoking, exercise, and cholesterol,[35] but very little mention has been made concerning human contact, even though several studies suggest the value of touch for treating the disease. These include the Framingham study, which showed that married couples live longer lives, whereas single and widowed people have shortened lives,[36] and similar data from both a 1956 study by Kraus and Lillienfeld[37] and a 1970 study by Carter and Glick.[38] Dr. Older claims that for every major cause of death—heart disease, homicide, stroke, cirrhosis of the liver, automobile accidents—divorced men stand a two to six times greater chance of dying than married men.[39] (Studies on the bereaved of these men show they also have increased illnesses and mortality rates from accidents and diseases.) Married and unmarried men may also, of course, differ in diet, exercise, and verbal interaction, but the physical contact variable is critical, perhaps because it reduces stress hormones and stimulates the immune system in the case of disease prevention, and enhances alertness in the case of accident prevention.

Jim Burke (former Chairman and CEO of Johnson & Johnson, current president of the Partnership for a Drug-Free America, and recipient of the Presidential Medal of Freedom on August 9, 2000) highlights the importance of touch in disease prevention,

The way to define health is "the absence of disease." I think the prevention of disease will happen through touch [and] I think you are going to be able to find ways to prove that in animal and human models. Unfortunately, there are a lot of people in our society, for example, children, who are emotionally deprived, deprived of touch. I think you are going to find that there are whole sets of diseases that come from touch deprivation. . . . I think we will develop models suggesting that we can enhance the immune system by touch. I have no doubt that people who are well-loved from birth to death have less disease. I would bet everything I own on that.[40]

5

Touch Messages to the Brain

Without a sense of touch, moving about in the world would be impossible. We usually think it is our hands that give us the most touch information because we use them to manipulate objects, but everything we do, including sitting, walking, kissing, and feeling pain, depends on touch. This becomes clear when we try to negotiate a slippery street, an icy ski slope, or a rocky terrain. Learning whether something is rough or smooth, cold or hot is critical in order to avoid splinters and burns. And, without the sensation of touch, the pleasure of skin-to-skin contact, or feeling velvet, or petting animals would be gone.

Touch is defined as the stimulation of the skin by thermal, mechanical, chemical, or electrical stimuli. All these stimuli cause changes in the skin that give us such sensations as pressure, warmth, and vibration, even though, after a day spent hitting the keys of a computer, pushing a pen, or just wearing our clothes, we tend to become less aware of these sensations. To understand the various functions of touch, it is important to understand the physical components of the skin and how the stimulation signals get conveyed from the skin to the brain.

Skin and Its Functions

The skin is the largest, oldest, and most sensitive sense organ in the body. Our whole body is covered and protected by our skin, even to the transparent cornea of the eye, which is covered by a layer of skinlike cells. Without skin we could not survive, and yet, except for diseases of the skin, skin is the most ignored organ. Even though the world has many research institutes for seeing and hearing, there are few for touching, with the result that there has been little research on touch and its stimulation of the skin.

Touch has been called "the mother of the senses," perhaps because it was the first to develop in evolution. Montagu notes that the word "touch" is the longest entry (fourteen full columns) in the *Oxford English Dictionary*, which defines it as "the most general of the bodily senses, diffused through all parts of skin, but (in man) specially developed in the tips of the fingers and the lips."[1] It is interesting that the fingers and lips have a disproportionately large number of nerves that travel to and from the brain, because they are the means by which the parent comes to know the newborn and the means by which the infant does most of its early learning. The *Dictionary of the Russian Language* says, "In reality all five senses can be reduced to one—the sense of touch. The tongue and palate sense the food; the ear, sound waves; the nose, emanation; the eyes, rays of light."[2]

Touch is the earliest sensory system to develop in all animal species. When a human embryo is less than an inch long and less than two months old, the skin is already highly developed. At two months gestation, the fingers will grasp when the palm is touched; at three months the fingers and thumb will close.

The skin and the nervous system arise from the same embryonic cell layer, the ectoderm, which is the outermost of three

cell layers. The central nervous system develops in the ectoderm as the internal portion of the general surface of the
embryonic body. After the differentiation of the brain and
spinal cord, the rest of the embryo's surface covering, the ectoderm, becomes the skin, hair, nails, and teeth, and gives rise to
the sense organs of hearing, smell, taste, vision, and touch. We
could consider the skin an exposed portion of the nervous
system or an external nervous system.[3] Touch can have strong
effects on our bodies because, when the skin is touched, that
stimulation is quickly transmitted to the brain, which in turn
regulates our bodies. Depending upon the type of touch we
receive, we can either be calmed down or aroused.

Physically, skin comprises about 18 percent of our body,
weighs approximately nine pounds, and is approximately eighteen square feet in area. A section of skin the size of a quarter
features a few million cells, a few hundred sweat glands, fifty
nerve endings, and three feet of blood vessels. In addition to
its critical function of holding in our organs, the skin protects
our bodies from dehydration, physical injury, toxic substances,
and ultraviolet radiation; it does this by perceiving these effects
and signaling the person to move away from the potentially
harmful exposure. Skin is waterproof and helps regulate our
body temperatures, as well as our water and salt metabolism,
by perspiration.[4] The skin also helps prevent disease by releas-
ing immune hormones. Its sebaceous glands help lubricate the
skin, particularly the lips, breasts, and genitalia. As a sense
organ, our skin is critical for perceiving and processing the
meaning of different touch stimuli. The ridges and valleys in
our highly sensitive fingertips are critical for the perception of
texture. Yet, despite all these functions, the skin is often taken
for granted unless it is burned or wounded.

The outermost layer of skin, the epidermis, can be thick or
thin, hairy or smooth, loose or tight, flat or furrowed. The

skin's surface contains many dead cells that get sloughed off every few hours as the outer layer of skin is replaced by a completely new layer. Skin cells shed at the rate of more than a million every hour;[5] to see this happen, apply a piece of Scotch tape to your skin, pull it off, and then note the cloudiness caused by the skin cells stuck to the tape.

Beneath this outermost epidermis is the dermis, which contains connective and nutritive tissues (figure 5.1). There are also

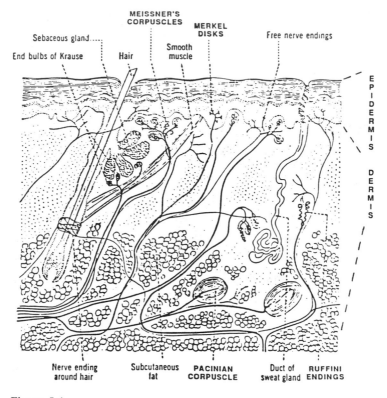

Figure 5.1
Schematic of the layers of human skin. From Heller, M. A., and Schiff, W. (eds.). (1991). *The Psychology of Touch*. Lawrence Erlbaum.

many specialized nerve cells in different layers of the skin that are named after their discoverers.[6] These structures are responsible for conveying the nerve signals from thermal, mechanical, chemical, and electrical stimuli. Meissner's corpuscles, located between the epidermis and the dermis on the hairless parts of the body—fingertips, palms, soles of the feet, tongue, sexual parts, and so on—respond to the lightest forms of stimulation. The Pacinian corpuscles, located near the joints and deep tissues and in the genitals and mammary glands, respond to pressure, vibrations, and high-frequency sounds. Merkel's disks, located just beneath the skin, respond to constant pressure. Ruffini endings, located deep in the skin, can also register pressure and temperature.

Messages to the Brain

The term *touch* includes several tactile senses: pressure, pain, temperature, and muscle movements. Any stimulation that touches the skin is carried to the spinal cord on nerve fibers that are sometimes no longer than several feet. These nerve fibers are small if they carry pain and temperature information, and large if they carry mechanical information up the spinal cord to the brain.

The information traveling to the brain ultimately crosses the sensory cortex to the opposite side of the brain where it is processed. Scientists have done experiments by placing electrodes on the surface of a person's cortex to note exactly where the brain receives and processes skin stimulation. A diagram of where the stimulation from different parts of the body is received by the brain is called a homunculus (figure 5.2). This diagram shows that, in determining how much space is needed on the cortex, the size of the body part is less important than the density of its nerves. Areas with many more nerve endings,

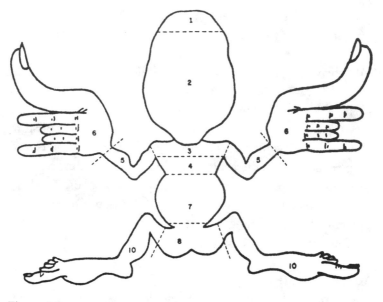

Figure 5.2
"Homunculus," a representation of the area on the cortex that receives and sends messages to different body parts. From Heller, M. A., and Schiff, W. (eds.). (1991). *The Psychology of Touch.* Lawrence Erlbaum.

such as our fingertips, lips, and genitals, require more space in the cortex than our back, which has far fewer nerve endings. In addition, the highly specialized nerve cells in the cortex are so sensitive to specific types of stimulation that some cells may, for example, be sensitive only to stroking the surface of a body part in one single direction, or at a specific frequency. Different types of stimulation can alter the size of these cells in the cortex, as well as the number of cells responding to the different types of stimulation.

Thresholds for Tactile Stimulation
Researchers use brush bristles and air puffs to produce sensations of pressure and vibration in order to determine a person's

response to the frequency, intensity, and temperature of tactile stimulus. One popular measure is how far apart two touch points must be for a person to perceive them as separate. The skin is touched with one or two brush hairs, and the person is asked to indicate the number of points felt. In sensitive areas the subject more readily perceives the two points. As we said, there is more sensitivity in parts of the body (fingertips, lips, and genitals, for example) that have more nerve endings. These areas are not only the most sensitive ones for perceiving temperature, texture, and other tactile stimulation, they also are the most sensitive to pain. To determine pain thresholds, experimenters push a dolorimeter (a rod that exerts pressure) against the skin. Using this device, wide differences in individuals' pain thresholds have been found.

Thermal Regulation

Survival would not be possible without thermal regulation. An increase of only three to four degrees in skin temperature causes a feeling of extreme heat. Similarly, to experience terrible cold, the skin temperature only needs to drop one to two degrees. We experience our lowest temperature at about 4:00 A.M., which is when, because of the dramatic change in our body's temperature, many asthma attacks occur.

Injury from freezing or burning can be avoided by escaping the extreme temperature, or by the body's dilating or constricting blood vessels, which leads to sweating or shivering. People are slow to notice injury from freezing, but being burned leads to an immediate reaction.[7] The transitions from warm to cold and cold to warm, such as moving out of the heat into a swimming pool, or moving out of the winter cold into a sauna, are pleasant thermal changes, perhaps because they neutralize the discomfort of extreme cold or extreme heat.[8] The body parts we leave the most exposed to the world when the body is fully clothed (the face, arms, and hands) are the ones that are the most sensitive to temperature changes. Those sensitive parts protect the body from frostbite and burns.

The Use of Touch in Devices for Seeing and Hearing

Sensory aids have been developed for the blind and the deaf using vibrating stimulation. Vibrations can relay pattern information about visual or auditory stimuli to the skin. The optacon is an example of this kind of device.[9] It consists of five rows of twenty pins that vibrate on a blind person's fingers to transmit patterns filmed by a small camera. The images transmitted from the camera through the vibrators pass from right to left under the reader's fingers as the reader moves his or her fingers across the page. This is useful because most printed information has not been translated into Braille. Blind people can read at speeds of sixty or more words per minute on the optacon.

Another device, called the tactile-visual substitution system, converts television scenes to tactile images,[10] which are represented by 400 individual vibrators that act as if they are imprinting the shapes of the images on the back of a blind person. One investigator reported that, as the camera rapidly zoomed in on the subject, the subject avoided it as if it was a looming object. This device has only been moderately successful.

Aids for the deaf are being researched more actively and are perhaps more effective than the vibrating devices for the blind at this time. Called tactile vocoders, they work by using multiple vibrators to translate vocal information into tactile stimulation. Tactile vocoders transmit sound to the skin of a deaf person in patterns of stimulation that closely approximate the sounds. The vocoders take the sound in through a microphone, divide it into a number of frequency bands, and then use that information to drive the stimulator on the skin, which then feeds tickle-like sensations to the skin through a belt worn on the arm, leg, abdomen, hand, or forehead. When a deaf person puts on this belt, the vibrators representing low-frequency sounds might start from the left of the belt, for example; the vibrators then convey different frequency sounds across the belt to the right end of the belt. According to Kim Oller at the Mailman Center for Child Development, deaf children learn to recognize the particular low and high frequency sounds and eventually learn to match those to the vibrations they feel when they speak into the device themselves.[11] As the sounds change, one can learn a systematic pattern. The information provided by the tactile vocoder tends to complement that provided by hearing aids and lip reading.

The cochlear implant is another device that may be effective. It can stimulate the acoustic nerve with electrical signals delivered by a microprocessor implanted beneath the skin in the person's head. An external microphone and an electrical device transmit this acoustic signal to the implanted microprocessor. Deaf people who lost their hearing after they learned to speak can carry on telephone conversations following cochlear implants.

These, then, are some of the ways the skin and the sense of touch can help us in the world. The sense of touch helps us avoid pain and drastic temperature changes, experience pleasurable sensations, navigate through space, perceive objects we manipulate, and sometimes helps to substitute for our other senses.

Touch for Pain Relief

Pain, particularly chronic pain, is one of the worst experiences in life, but touch can help to relieve it by blocking the pain messages. This is possible because the touch signals travel to the brain faster than the pain signals.

The pain experience is complex, and pain sensations differ in many ways, including in their duration, intensity, location, and quality. The McGill Pain Questionnaire, from McGill University in Montreal, describes pain with as many as 200 pain-related adjectives using spatial, temporal, thermal, and pressure characteristics[12]—burning, cramping, pounding, stabbing, and stinging are just a few of these. Pain due to back injuries, headaches, or stomachaches is different from pain due to burns. Chronic pain is different from transient pain, and isolated pain is different from widespread pain. An often-noted curious phenomenon is that people who are in accidents rarely complain about pain until several hours later. Even more surprising are the initiation rituals in many non-industrial cultures that do not seem to cause pain, like walking on hot coals, or receiving puncture wounds from ceremonial implements.

People used to think pain was received by specific receptors, but the current thinking is that pain is received by the brain generally, as no specific sense organ for touch (such as the retina for vision) exists. Alleviating or removing pain with pharmacological or surgical procedures is difficult, but simple natural treatments are often effective. A classic example is the relief felt after putting an injured area under cold water or applying a warm cloth and massaging it; dipping the area in cold water or rubbing it stimulates many more nerves, which could partially explain why the pain is relieved.

Therapies for Pain Reduction

Doctors Melzack and Wall formulated the gate control theory of pain to explain why acupuncture, massages, rubbing, and other forms of pressure stimulation might alleviate pain.[13] Their theory suggests that information passing through the spinal cord is like an object passing through a gate. If the gate is open, the pain message is allowed to flow uninterrupted, but if the gate is partly or completely closed, then the pain message can be interrupted and the pain is not experienced. For example, messages from longer, more insulated nerve fibers, such as those for pressure, can be transmitted to the brain faster than the shorter, less insulated nerve fibers for pain can, in effect closing the gate to the slower pain messages. Temperature stimuli such as heat and cold can also reach the brain faster because temperature fibers are also longer and more insulated than the pain fibers. The essence of the gate control theory is that the messages from the heat and cold or the pressure that we apply to painful areas reach the brain faster than the pain message, thus preventing the pain message from being received.

Massages used to be one of the primary ways of treating pain, but the advent of pharmaceuticals—particularly opiate drugs—in the 1940s replaced massages for pain treatment. Unfortunately, manufactured opiate drugs have many side effects, including constipation, nausea, respiratory depression, and, too often, dependence on the drug. Fortunately, though, the body can also produce natural opiates as morphine-like chemicals. The pain-relieving effects of these natural painkillers, called endorphins (or beta endorphins, dynorphins, or enkephalins), and other pain-relieving brain chemicals such as serotonin can be further augmented by electrical stimulation with a transcutaneous electrical nerve stimulation

(TENS) device that transmits small amounts of electrical current into the body[14] through a metal rod about the size of a pen. Aerobic exercise is another way to produce the painkilling endorphins.

The neurotransmitter serotonin is the base for many drugs used to treat chronic pain in migraine headaches and depression. Eating certain foods—for example milk and bananas, which are high in tryptophan (a precursor of serotonin)—can also reduce pain. Albert Schweitzer expressed amazement that the African patients at his village hospital had very high pain thresholds and were never depressed; it could have been because their diet was rich in bananas.

Chronic Pain
Chronic pain is pain that lasts longer than six months. People with chronic pain become depressed due to the ineffectiveness of the drugs they are taking and the dramatic changes in lifestyle they experience. People with the chronic pain of migraine headaches or fibromyalgia (pain all over the body for no known reason) seem to have low endorphin levels, which could be the reason for their chronic pain syndrome. Or alternatively, any related nerve damage could have consumed their body's supply of natural painkilling opiates and reduced the effectiveness of their natural endorphins. Conversely, there are those rare people who are insensitive to pain, which may be due to a pain-transmission problem or to an overabundance of endorphins.

Most chronic pain disorders are unresponsive to surgical, pharmacological, or other medical interventions, making the use of touch and pressure treatments (acupuncture, acupressure, massage therapy, etc.) for severe chronic pain very important. These therapies may be effective because they lower anxiety levels, which tend to aggravate pain, or because they release painkilling endorphins and serotonin, or because they stimulate the longer nerve fibers that transmit their signals to the brain faster than the shorter pain signals.

Touch for Stress Reduction
Chronic stress is another source of pain. Touch has been rediscovered as an effective therapy for healthy, drug-free relief from stress. For this, we can thank the health, fitness, wellness, stress-reduction, and alternative medicine movements, which have all been instrumental in reviving the old forms of treatment for stress.

Massage therapy is an effective technique for stress reduction. Stresses created by our fast-moving lifestyles, our jobs, and our relationships cause muscle tension and respiratory and cardiovascular problems. Under stress, we experience an increased heart rate and elevated blood pressure and stress hormone levels (e.g., norepinephrine and cortisol), as well as a decreased blood flow to the digestive tract, the extremities, and the immune system. As the stress continues, we often self-medicate with alcohol and prescription or other drugs to reduce the aches and pains, fatigue, headaches, indigestion, insomnia, lack of appetite, overeating, or other stress symptoms we are experiencing. We need some form of relaxation to alleviate these problems. In addition to massage therapy, such relaxation techniques as exercise, imagery, meditation, music, progressive muscle relaxation, and yoga can also slow our bodies down when we are stressed.

Massage therapy can significantly alleviate job stress. Instead of coffee breaks or martini lunches, many corporations and law firms offer office-chair massages during the lunch hour as part of their wellness programs. The typical office massage is conducted at a desk chair or a specially designed massage chair that looks like an ergonomics stool but which also has a chest brace and a doughnut-shaped face brace. The massage takes about ten or fifteen minutes and costs about a dollar a minute. People seem to like these massages, and comment positively on them in surveys, saying, "the massage makes me more alert," or "my energy level has increased."

We recently conducted a study on job stress that confirms these impressions.[15] In this study, twenty employees of the University of Miami Medical School each received a fifteen-minute massage twice a week for a month during their lunch hour. Immediately following the massage, the employees said they felt less anxiety and were in a better state of mind. As compared to a group who simply relaxed, they also showed greater alertness after the massages and were able to perform math computations in half the time with half the errors. Our study further noted long-term changes, including lower levels of the stress hormone cortisol and lower levels of norepinephrine and depression. Recently, a business called "The Great American Backrub" capitalized on these benefits in busy urban areas like New York City by setting up a series of fast massage shops that featured pneumatic chairs designed to measure and adjust to your body frame for the perfect job-stress massage. There are similar chairs at "Unwind" on the beach in Hollywood, Florida, and in airports such as the Seattle airport's "Massage Bar."

Massage therapy also reduces other forms of stress; for example, pregnancy and delivery stress can be reduced by having the woman's partner provide a gentle massage. As the data suggest, massage stimulates the parasympathetic nervous system, which then slows the body down and increases attentiveness. That may, in turn, relax the sympathetic nervous system, which arouses the nervous system when the body needs to be active. During emergencies, your sympathetic nervous system is activated; during a learning task, your parasympathetic system is activated. The changes that occur in your body during a massage—your heart rate and your stress hormones slowing down, for example—help to lessen the wear and tear on your body's organs and its immune system. In addition to all this, the massage and the resulting decrease in stress simply feel good, a pleasure we all deserve.

6

Touch Therapies

We can classify touch therapies into three groups: energy methods, manipulative therapies, and amalgams (combinations of both). All of these alternative medical therapies are becoming increasingly popular. A recent *New England Journal of Medicine* article by D. M. Eisenberg and his colleagues from Harvard reported survey data suggesting that as many as 33 percent of the American people are paying for alternative medicine out of their own pockets because it is not covered by most health care plans. In this survey, the most popular forms of alternative medicine were chiropractic care, massage therapy, and relaxation therapy.[1] Because there are so few data on the relative effectiveness of these therapies, most people tend to try a therapist who has been recommended and find a preferred therapy by trial and error.

Energy Methods

Acupressure, acupuncture, reflexology, tai chi chuan, and yoga are referred to as energy methods. All involve stimulating body points to move energy throughout the body.

Tai Chi Chuan, Yoga

In many primitive tribes, as well as most Eastern cultures, health is seen as the movement of energy through the body via meridians or channels. The Chinese call this energy *qi*, or *chi* (pronounced "chee"). Acupuncture or acupressure can manipulate chi points along the meridians so that the chi energy "flows freely." Some people practice tai chi (pronounced "ty chee"), a combination of exercise and meditation, to keep their energy flowing freely. It has become increasingly popular in the United States as an exercise technique that strengthens the legs and helps coordination. Recent research suggests less lower back pain,[2] less arthritis pain,[3] and better balance[4] in senior citizens after a course of tai chi. In addition, in recent tai chi studies there was an improvement in the gait of senior citizens[5] and there was more on-task behavior in adolescents with attention deficit hyperactivity disorder.[6]

People from some Eastern cultures believe that the universal energy that comes from the environment is channeled into our bodies by the food we eat and the air we breathe. That is why yoga emphasizes deep breathing, and why energy therapists claim they can treat stress-related problems, addictions, and pain of many kinds. Again, there has been very little research conducted on these methods, and the underlying mechanisms to explain how they work have not yet been discovered, although energy methods have certainly withstood the test of time in Eastern cultures, where they have been used for thousands of years.

Yoga and tai chi have many features in common with massage therapy. For example, yoga can be a form of self-massage, inasmuch as limbs are pressed up against each other and against a floor surface. In that sense it may be that, like massaging, yoga stimulates pressure receptors (specialized nerve endings that respond to pressure and other sensory stimuli), which would increase the activity of the vagus nerve (the cranial nerve that supplies sensation throughout much of the body) and thereby slow the body down and enhance attentiveness. In the same way that massage therapy reduces pain, the stimulation of pressure receptors (the long, more insulated nerve fibers for pressure) may also reduce pain.

Acupressure and Acupuncture
The channels or meridians through which electrical energy passes in the Eastern systems have corresponding points on the surface of the skin, which skin can be pressed or punctured to affect the workings of internal organs or to enhance pain tolerance—pressing a point on the forearm is said to reduce lower back pain, for example. Each meridian has an entry point at the skin's surface where the energy enters and an exit point where the energy leaves. These meridians are a kind of road map (which is what they look like on the charts; see figure 6.1).

The Japanese version of acupressure is called shiatsu ("shi" for finger and "atsu" for pressure). Shiatsu therapists use prolonged and heavy pressure; because of this, the therapy is painful for some, though not for others. The Shiatsu practitioner primarily uses the balls of his or her thumbs and occasionally the palms or the elbows, and follows a diagram of the key pressure points called *tsubos* (the points on the skin where the energy enters the meridians). Therapists have provided various theories for the shiatsu effects, including an increase in vagal activity (slowing of the heart caused by the vagus nerve), which would relax the patient. Others suggest that stress and muscle spasms might be reduced by the increased glucose released into the body by the strong massaging.

Tradition says that, in ancient times, Eastern therapists used only their fingers (acupressure) to manipulate chi, and that

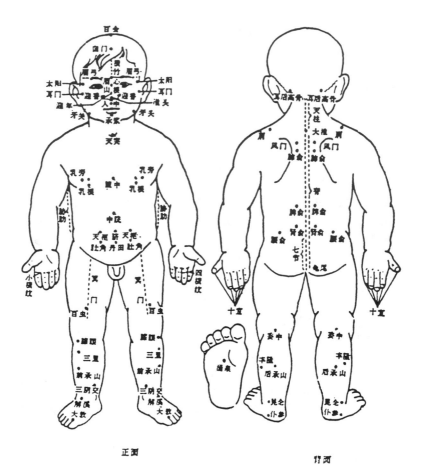

Figure 6.1
Ancient Chinese drawing of the meridians or sensory channels
throughout the body. From Flaws, B. (1985). *Turtle Tail and Other
Tender Mercies: Traditional Chinese Pediatrics.* Blue Poppy Press.

needles came in later to intensify the effects. Acupuncture requires considerable training and experience to be able to place the needles accurately.[1] Those undergoing acupuncture treatments feel only a minor pinprick, like a mosquito bite lasting only two or three seconds. Most acupuncturists use about 100 to 150 body points for needle insertion. Part of their skill is knowing which of these to select as the best treatment for each individual's condition. Acupuncture has been effectively used to treat many forms of addiction (drug abuse, alcoholism, overeating), and for the treatment of several diseases, including arthritis and hypertension. Medical schools are beginning to offer educational programs in acupuncture, and its use is also increasing in major teaching hospitals during surgery or childbirth. The National Institutes of Health recently explored the effects of acupuncture with a task force that concluded that it was an effective treatment for pain disorders. The Institute for Complementary and Alternative Medicine at the NIH recognizes it as an alternative therapy for pain syndromes. Acupuncture is one of the most popular alternative therapies, along with chiropractic and massage. It is often favored over Western anesthesia because it does not lower blood pressure or depress breathing. Other acupuncture-like stimulation is being explored, including water injections, laser beams, and sonar rays.[8] How these would block pain is as mysterious right now as the acupuncture needles themselves.

Reflexology

Reflexology is another energy method, although it could be called a massage therapy because it involves kneading, stroking, rubbing, and other massage procedures, centered on particular points of the ears, feet, or hands. According to reflexologists, energy from the point that is touched is transmitted across a network of nerves to other parts of the body, such as the back or the stomach.

The feet and hands are considered the connection to the rest of the body so that, for example, a touch at a certain point on the heel affects the lower back (figure 6.2). The middle of the foot is connected to the stomach area, the ball of the foot is connected to the heart and lungs, the toes are connected to the head, eyes, and mouth, and so on. Again, very little is known about the origins of this therapy, and there are no empirical data on the use of this method, but it works.

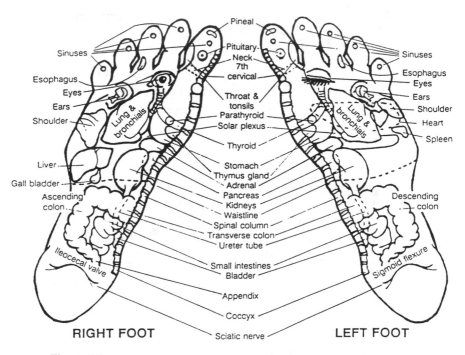

Figure 6.2
Ancient Chinese drawing of the pressure points on the feet. From Owens, M. K., and Ehrenreich, D. (1991). Application of nonpharmacologic methods of managing chronic pain. *Holistic Nursing Practice* 6: 32–40. © 1991, Aspen Publishers, Inc.

A curious finding resulted from a recent study we were conducting on providing pregnant women massage therapy. Although the fetus is not noted to respond to stimulation on the mother's abdomen with a vibrator (or similar stimulation) until approximately 24 weeks gestation, we noted fetal movement in response to the mothers' receiving foot massage as early as twenty weeks. This suggests that stimulating of pressure receptors in the feet somehow conveys messages to the uterus to elicit activity in the fetus. We are now conducting research to determine if similar kinds of stimulation to the hand creates a similar response.

Manipulative Therapies

Manipulative therapies include chiropractic care, massage therapy, osteopathy, and the Trager method, which all involve movement of muscle tissue.

Massage Therapy
As already mentioned, medicine essentially consisted of touch therapies before the advent of pharmaceutical drugs. The "laying-on of hands" was the primary form of healing throughout history in many places, including in ancient Greece, where Hippocrates, the father of modern medicine, wrote that "the physician must be experienced in many things, most especially in rubbing."[9]

Eastern touch therapies have been practiced for thousands of years, but they have only recently reached the Western world. The beginnings of Western massage date back to Peter Lind, an athlete and educator from nineteenth-century Sweden; his Swedish massage technique is one of the most popular touch therapies in the Western countries. The various forms of massage therapy practiced in different countries are now considered a form of medical treatment, for example, in China, Japan, Russia, and West Germany (among other countries), where it is covered by national health insurance, but in the United States, massage therapy is still considered an alternative medicine. Nonetheless, its popularity seems to be growing, judging from how many national and international massage therapy associations have increased their membership rolls by literally thousands of therapists in the last ten years.

According to its practitioners, massage therapy, in addition to "feeling good," releases muscle tension, facilitates the removal of toxic metabolic waste products resulting from exercise or inactivity, and allows more nutrients and oxygen to reach the body's cells and tissues (table 6.1). Practitioners also say that massage therapy is accompanied by the release of endorphins (the body's natural painkillers), and we know from our own research that massage therapy increases natural killer cells (enhancing the immune system's functioning).[10]

Swedish massage, the most common form of massage in this country, is usually given on a massage table, on the floor, or on a special massage chair, and often with oil (aromatic, baby, or vegetable oil), which is stroked and kneaded into all parts of the body. Swedish massage is generally divided into six types, in order of increasing pressure applied: (1) stroking or effleurage; (2) friction, moving the hands over the body with more pressure than stroking; (3) pressure without movement; (4) kneading or petrissage, where the hands are stationary, but the fingers move, working their way into sore muscles; (5) vibration, where a machine is generally used instead of human touch; and (6) percussion, a combination of slapping, pounding, and tapping.

Smooth stroking (called effleurage) and kneading (petrissage) movements are done up and down the back, across the shoulder and neck muscles, and on the backs of the legs, feet, arms,

Table 6.1
Massage therapy effects reported by massage therapists

Physical Level
Deep relaxation and stress reduction
Relief of muscle tension and stiffness
Reduced muscle spasm and tension
Greater joint flexibility and range of motion
Increased ease and efficiency of movement
Deeper and easier breathing promoted
Better circulation of both blood and lymph fluids
Reduced blood pressure
Relief of tension-related headaches, eyestrain
Healthier, better nourished skin
Improved posture
Faster healing time from pulled muscles and sprained ligaments;
reduced spasm, pain, and swelling; reduced formation of scar tissue
Strengthened immune system and disease prevention
Health maintenance

Mental Level
Relaxed state of alertness
Reduced mental stress; a calmer mind
Greater ability to monitor stress signals and respond appropriately
Increased capacity for clearer thinking

Emotional Level
Satisfying the need for caring and nurturing touch
Feeling of well-being
Greater ease of emotional expression
Enhanced self-image
Reduced levels of anxiety
Increased awareness of the mind-body connection
A sense of being unified and in harmony

and hands. Smooth stroking is also done on the front, across the stomach, the front of the legs and arms, and the face and forehead. According to its practitioners, Swedish massage boosts circulation by sending more blood to the muscles, and it facilitates oxygen consumption and waste elimination in the muscles.[11]

The Trager Method

The Trager method, named after its founder, involves gently holding and rocking different body parts. For example, the arms and legs are separately suspended to the side or above the body, and then softly rocked back and forth. This is a very gentle form of body work, and for people with generalized pain, this method may be preferable because no pressure is applied to the painful tissues.

Osteopathy

Osteopathy is considered an alternative form of medicine, but the training of osteopaths is very similar to that of MDs, both in curriculum and rigor. Osteopaths manipulate soft and connective tissues to balance the tendons, muscles, and ligaments attached to bones. They place tension on joints by moving a limb back and forth until they hear a clicking or popping sound as the osteopath works to correctly align the body so that the joints no longer feel abnormal pressures. Osteopaths also treat with medication and focus on lifestyle habits such as nutrition. They are more prevention-oriented than orthodox MDs, who are more treatment-oriented.

Chiropractic Care

Chiropractors also focus on lifestyle, including exercise and diet, but they are more concerned with adjusting the spinal column. According to chiropractors, many of the thirty-three vertebrae in the spinal column need to be realigned if they are obstructing an opening in the vertebrae that the nerves pass through, or if they are pressing on an adjacent nerve and causing pain. Chiropractic care is reminiscent of the practice in Tonga where children trampled on people for manipulative therapy, and in China where it was not surprising to see massage therapists hanging from horizontal overhead poles as they walked across the backs of their clients.

Amalgams

Several forms of touch therapy are an amalgamation of energy and manipulative therapies, or combinations of mind/body work.

Chinese Massage
Chinese massage is an example of an ancient technique that combines massage and acupressure. As with acupressure or shiatsu, the therapist applies pressure along the meridians.

Polarity Therapy
Polarity therapy is another technique that combines several touch therapies, including energy, manipulation, massage, and postural techniques. In this therapy, which is based on energy flow, the body is divided into poles similar to a magnet, with the top of the body and the right side of the body being positively charged, and the bottom of the body, the feet, and the left side being negatively charged.[12] Polarity therapists suggest that there are different centers in the body that regulate different functions. One center regulates hearing and speaking, another the circulatory and respiratory systems, a third the digestive system, and so on. The therapy includes deep

pressure and stretching moves intended to release any energy blockages.

Reichian Massage

Reichian massage is still another example of an amalgamation of massage and energy techniques. Wilhelm Reich, who was a disciple of Freud during the psychoanalytic movement, decided that a new therapy that worked on both the body and mind simultaneously was needed, something he called "psychoanalysis that includes body work."[13] He believed that neuroses and most physical disorders sprang from an energy blockage. If you block your feelings, his theory went, your muscles must defend against your emotions, and this interrupts the flow of energy. Reich believed that each region of the body was associated with a different emotion, so the Reichian therapist kneads, pokes, and occasionally strokes, in a kind of rough-looking massage, the different parts of the body that the emotion is blocking. Other Reichian techniques include venting the emotions by crying, kicking, pounding, and screaming. Talk therapy is, of course, included in this mind-body therapy as well. Reich also developed the "orgone box," which was designed to attract energy; his patients could sit in this human-size box and benefit from the energy healing it provided.

The Feldenkrais Technique

The Feldenkrais technique is intended to improve posture and the individual's awareness of his or her movements and gestures. Feldenkrais believed that the body reflects what is happening in the mind, and vice versa.[14] Various gentle manipulative techniques are used, along with movement intended to increase body awareness. These movements are very small and subtle, like turning the head or lifting the arm over and over. According to this method, constantly repeating a good posture movement enables people to replace their bad posture movement. For example, if they keep their arms stiffly by their sides rather than loosely swinging them during walking, they will learn the more beneficial loose swinging by repeating that exercise while walking.

Applied Kinesiology

Applied kinesiology combines a number of these other methods. This form of therapy is derived from the study of the muscles and their functions, where on a bone a muscle originates or attaches, and where on a bone it ends. Kinesiologists can diagnose weakened muscles by probing the body and feeling the muscles during different movements,[15] usually isometric ones. They then use a combination of osteopathic, chiropractic, muscle manipulation, and exercise techniques to restore the muscle strength. Many chiropractors and osteopaths use applied kinesiology for alleviating painful conditions in the muscles, joints, ligaments, and so on. Many people who need to keep their muscles in top condition also use it.

Massage Therapy Amalgam

The massage therapy amalgam we have come to use for children and adults in our research studies at the Touch Research Institutes and our *Unwind* wellness centers was designed by Iris Burman, Director of the *Educating Hands Massage Therapy Institute* in Miami. See boxes 6.1 and 6.2.

Box 6.1
Table Massage

The typical table massage requires another person to administer the massage. These instructions are for the massage therapist.

Supine (face up)—fifteen minutes

Head/Neck

1. *Traction neck:* Place your fingertips evenly under the ridge at the base of the person's neck, allowing the head to rest in the palm of your hand as you press gently into the vertebrae with your fingertips. Then pull gently on the neck to lengthen spine.

2. *Stroke the neck:* With the flat of your hand, stroke one side of the neck from head to shoulder. Repeat on the other side.

3. *Lateral forehead stroking:* Place the palms of both your hands on the forehead, stroke outward toward the temple.

4. *Temporomandibular joint (TMJ):* With your fingertips, give slow elliptical strokes to the jaw joint. Continue with your fingertips and stretch the muscle overlying the jaw joint from the cheekbone to the lower jaw region.

5. *Depress the shoulder:* Place the palms of your hands on the tops of the shoulders and press down evenly toward the feet. Hold for about thirty seconds. Add a little rocking movement.

6. *Mid-shoulder trigger point:* Place your thumbs in the hollow at the top of the shoulders. A trigger point lies in this area, and it may be sensitive. If so, press only as deeply as the person can tolerate. Depress this mid-shoulder trigger point for one minute.

Arms

7. *Traction arms:* Supporting the elbow and the hand, gently pull (traction) the person's arm down toward the feet. Maintaining the traction, move the arm through its natural range of shoulder motion, up and over the head and out to the side.

8. *Massage hands:* Apply gentle squeezing motions to the entire hand and make friction movements on the palm of the hand.

9. *Massage the arm:* Give long, slow gliding strokes from the hand up and over the shoulder. Repeat seven times.

10. *Shoulder stroke:* With the flat of your hand, give slow, rounding strokes, encircling the shoulder. Repeat seven times.

11. *Hold Hoku point:* Gently squeeze the fleshy part of the webbing that lies between the thumb and the forefinger (the Hoku point) for about one minute. This area may be tender, so press only as deeply as the person can tolerate.

Torso
12. *Rocking the rib cage:* Hold the ribs on both sides and gently rock the rib cage side to side. This creates a gently relaxing wave through the body.

13. *Solar plexus hold:* Place one hand gently over the solar plexus (the diaphragm area just below the breastbone) and place your other hand over the forehead. Hold lightly while the person breathes into your hand. Add a gentle rocking motion.

Legs
14. *Traction legs:* Holding the ankles, keep the legs close together and pull them straight down, away from the body. Maintaining the traction, move the legs together, first to the left, then to the right.

15. *Massage the feet:* Apply gentle squeezing motions to the entire foot and make friction movements with your thumbs on the top of the foot, following the spaces between the bones with simple, slow, not digging movements. Press into the soles of the feet with your thumbs.

16. *Massage the leg:* Give long, slow gliding strokes from the foot to the hip. Repeat seven times.

Prone (face down)—fifteen minutes

Legs
17. *Achilles tendon stretch:* Lift the leg, bend the foot at the ankle, and stretch the back of the calf.

Continued

18. *Work the calf:* Stroke up the calf from the ankle to the knee. Squeeze the fleshy part of the calf.

19. *Thigh shake:* With the knee bent, place one hand over the thigh and shake the muscles gently.

20. *Stroking leg:* Make long strokes from the heel, up and over the buttocks.

Back

21. *Lateral lumbar stretch:* Drape your hands over the low back, putting the heel of your hands along the vertebral column. Gently press into the low back and stroke toward the sides of the body. Repeat ten times.

22. *Strokes parallel to the spine:* Putting your hands on each side of the spine, stroke firmly but gently all the way up to the shoulders and out the arms, connecting the low back to the arms.

23. *Trapezius squeeze:* Grasp the top of the shoulder and squeeze.

24. *Friction alongside the spine:* With the side edges of both hands on either side of the back, make friction movements from the top to the bottom of the back.

25. *Posterior neck squeeze and stretch:* Gently squeeze the soft tissue at the back of the neck. Stretch this area, pulling one hand toward the head and the other to the upper back.

26. *Sacral traction:* Place the heel of your hand at the very bottom of the back, just above the buttocks, and press gently while pushing the back toward the feet.

27. *Gentle rock:* Place one hand over the lumbar (lower back) region, the other hand over the upper back between the shoulder blades. Gently rock for twenty seconds and then hold still for a minute.

This procedure is slightly modified when working with difficult conditions such as lower back pain and migraine headaches.

Some of our studies, for example our job stress study, were performed using a chair massage. This procedure, also designed by Iris Burman, is as follows:

Box 6.2
Chair Massage

(NB: These are abbreviated instructions to a massage therapist, based on the fuller ones given for a table massage.)

Back
1. Compression to the back parallel to the spine from the shoulders to the base of the spine.
2. Compression to the entire back adding some gentle rock.
3. Trapezius squeeze.
4. Finger pressure around scapula and shoulder.
5. Finger pressure along the length of the spine and back.
6. Circular strokes to hips below iliac (pelvic) crest.

Arms
7. Drop arm to the side. Knead arm from shoulder to lower arm.
8. Press down points on upper and lower arm.

Hands
9. Massage entire hand. Traction to the fingers.
10. Hold Hoku point for fifteen to twenty seconds.
11. Traction of the arm. Lateral and superior. (Make sure arm is in line with the body.)

Neck/Back
12. Kneading of cervical vertebrae.
13. Finger pressure along base of skull (occipital bone) and along side of neck.
14. Scalp massage.

Continued

15. Press down on trapezius, finger pressure and squeezing continuing down the arm.

16. Close with light pounding, using small finger side of hands on shoulders and down the back.

Touch Therapies by Another Name

Many touch therapies go by another name. As Diane Ackerman notes in *A Natural History of the Senses*, "Touch is so powerful a healer that we go to professional touchers (doctors, hairdressers, masseuses, dance instructors, cosmeticians, barbers, gynecologists, chiropodists, tailors, back manipulators, prostitutes and manicurists) and frequent employers of touch—discotheques, shoeshine stands and mud baths."[16] It seems that, as our culture places more restrictions on touch within human relationships, alternative forms of touch become more popular. It is as if we needed a minimum of touch for our emotional well-being and physical wellness, so we find acceptable ways, and sometimes functional ways (e.g., going to the hairdresser), of being touched.

Touch Skincare

Several skincare businesses, including barbers, beauticians, hairdressers, manicurists, and pedicurists are providing touch therapy along with the skincare functions they perform. Some people say the scalp massage during the shampoo is the best part of their weekly visits to the hairdresser. For others, this weekly visit is the only occasion for being touched by another person. Increasingly, beauty salons feature massage chairs so touch can be applied to other parts of the body in addition to the head, hands, and feet. Some salons even provide infant massages while the new mother has a shampoo.

In Budapest, there is a touch spa on every corner. The people there claim that they are stress-free because they often have a facial and body massage on their way to work. In the United States, daily massages are considered by most people to be too expensive. Instead, body brushes and shower-head massaging devices have become increasingly popular as Americans attempt to provide their own touch therapies. A psychologist colleague recently asked half his depressed patients to brush themselves with a natural, longhandled brush from the natural food store when they take showers. Those who did so recovered from their depression sooner than those who did not.

Touch Toys

The market for touch toys is flourishing in this country. Touch toys constitute almost 30 percent of the inventory of popular mail-order catalog companies such as Brookstone, Hammacher-Schlemmer, Self-Care, and The Sharper Image. In these catalogues, you can find touch toys, ranging from pocket-sized to chair-sized massage devices to cover every part of the body, including foot-massage platforms, full undulating beds, neck-collar massage devices, reclining massage chairs, as well as massagers for the scalp, for shampooing, or for brushing teeth, and angular devices with moving parts to get to hard-to-reach parts of the body. Parents can even buy gum massagers to help their infants through teething. Brushes and combs alone were evidently not enough, it seems, so these highly specialized massaging devices also provide vibration and, in some cases, moisture and heat. Some are even advertised as shiatsu devices for providing deep-pressure massage.

Other touch toys, like Chinese metal balls, goosebump balls, silly putty, and stress-relieving squeezing toys, are popular. And, for driving to the office, there is even a massager/heater cushion you can sit on that can be activated by plugging it into an automobile cigarette lighter.

Touch Sports

Sports probably provide us with the greatest variety of touch stimulation. In sports we not only touch people, but also touch nature—the air, earth, and water around us. In many sports—jogging, running, diving, swimming, and surfing, for example—the touch sense becomes more sensitive because of the streams of air and water that run by us. But sadly, there is also that negative touch in sports—the kicking, punching, and ramming that goes along with contact sports such as football, soccer, and basketball. Although some would argue that these are healthy outlets for aggression, they also carry significant risks for dangerous outcomes such as broken bones, spinal cord injuries, and so forth.

Touch Dancing

Dancing in all its forms, including folk, square, and polka dancing, jigging, jitterbugging, ballroom, swing, and now line dancing are increasingly popular touch activities. Whereas the '60s and '70s featured the distant dancing of rock and roll, today, ballroom dancing, swing dancing, and touch dancing (all involving close body contact) are coming back. Perhaps they are again popular because other forms of physical intimacy have been lost with the AIDS epidemic and the fear of catching a disease from close contact.

Touch Games

Everywhere in the world children play "tag" instinctively, without being taught how. Rough and tumble play is something that comes naturally to children as soon as they walk. Before that, in the crawling stage, they approach and hug each other somewhat more clumsily. Some little kids even massage each other. A therapist recently saw a toddler in her classroom get up from a backrub, move over to another toddler, and proceed to give him a backrub. Similarly, after getting her hands rubbed, a preschooler started a chain of children massaging each other's hands. With American children as young as six being sent home from school for "sexual harassment" just for simply kissing each other on the cheek, it seems that children will need to be taught how they can and cannot touch their friends in order for touching to be acceptable in today's schools.

Touch games can be played in an organized fashion to encourage appropriate touch in the family and at school. The blindfold game is a good one for getting people to see how well they know each other. Each person gets blindfolded and then feels the hands, fingers, even face of the other person to try and guess who they are. Both at home and at school, anonymous backrubs can be given in a guessing game of who is doing it, or as a reward for finishing a job. For teachers, now more cautious about touching children because they fear accusations of sexual abuse, backrubs are an appropriate way to be affectionate. Student to student backrubs are also a nonpromiscuous way of making intimate contact. A favorite school-time massage is the massage train, where the class forms a large circle, with each person massaging the back of the person in front, and then switching the direction to massage the person on the other side (figure 6.3).

Jules Older teaches six different kinds of group-touch exercises in his lectures to free people up from their inhibitions about touching and being touched.[17] In the first, the standing person taps her or his fingertips rapidly and very lightly on the shoulders of her or his partner. This is called *snowflakes*. The next is *raindrops*. Here they tap their fingers simultaneously

Figure 6.3
Human massage train.

and with greater intensity. Then she/he *glides* across her/his partner's back, using the heels of the hands and parallel strokes. In the fourth, using hollow palms she/he claps her/his hands across the back and shoulders, creating the sound of *horse hooves*. The fifth stage is *whirlpools*, a penetrating massage of circling thumbs. Finally, the massage recipient is asked which touch was preferred and is then given an extra dose of that. Each stage lasts two or three minutes. When all six are done, the partners switch places and the sequence begins again.

Sex Touch Therapies

As mentioned earlier, Sensate Focus, developed by Masters and Johnson, is the best known of all sex therapy programs. Couples who participate in this two-week program are instructed "not to have sex," but simply to engage in a gentle touching program everywhere on the body except the genital and breast areas. Partners take turns touching and being touched. This program is designed to remove performance anxiety and to enhance arousal and the desire for sex. If a couple is still experiencing performance anxiety after trying this method, they might go on to try a more structured massage routine. Other exercises intended to provide anxiety-free intimacy include showering together, shampooing each other, bathing each other's feet, and washing each other's backs. Whether done formally in sex therapy or informally at home, these touch games can enhance sexual intimacy.

Self-Touch and Touch Objects

Several forms of self-touch and touch objects can also provide touch stimulation. A study was done in which newborns were placed on natural wool lambskins. The warm cozy lambskins provided stimulation that contributed to the newborns' gaining weight, made them less restless, and appeared to make them sleep better. In addition, when premature infants were placed on the lambskins, they showed less loss of body heat. We made the mistake of attempting this with artificial sheepskins and found that even the premature infants could pull out the fibers and stuff them in their mouths, which was potentially very dangerous.

Swaddling, when done correctly so as to inhibit limb movements, also provides constant touch stimulation that can be soothing. Elizabeth Anisfield has researched snugglies, the modern counterpart in the United States.[18] When compared to hard seat carriers, these soft baby carriers led to better interactions between the mothers and their infants. They verbalized to each other more often and were more responsive to each other in general. In these baby carriers, parents generally carry their infants facing in toward their chest, which usually puts the infants to sleep. In a recent study, we found that the infants also like facing outward to explore the passing world, particularly when they are not sleepy.

Researcher Betsy Lozoff found that, in nonindustrial societies, infants are continuously carried in a sling or pouch where the infant has easy access to breastfeeding.[19] The previously described (in chapter 3) kangaroo method of carrying the premature infant skin to skin, as if in a kangaroo pouch inside the parent's clothes, can also lead to greater infant weight gain and more rapid clinical improvement from prematurity and related medical problems. Objects such as cuddly stuffed animals (or even a real pet) and security blankets also give soothing touch stimulation, as do different kinds of self-stimulation such as sucking on a pacifier, thumb-sucking, rocking, and playing with the genitals.

A number of our studies show the positive effects of sucking on a pacifier during invasive procedures, ranging from weight gain to reduced crying and reduced stress hormone levels (cortisol).[20] Even though doctors and dentists continue to advise against pacifiers as bad for the development of straight teeth, pacifiers appear to have many more positive than negative effects.

Some bad habits, such as cuticle-picking, hair-stroking, nail-biting, and obsessive hand-scrubbing, could be classified as self-touch activities. Other bad habits are unfriendly touch gestures, such as folding your arms or drumming your fingers in an agitated way as you're listening to someone.

Although one touch gesture, masturbation, is considered a bad habit, it is actually a normal and healthy part of development. Sherrie Cohen, the author of *The Magic of Touch*, provides an anecdote to illustrate this point.[21] "One little eight-year-old boy was *comforting himself* one day, when his mother caught him. 'You'll go blind if you do that filthy thing!', she shrieked. The little boy stopped and thought about how good self-touch felt, then asked, 'Well, can I do it just till I have to wear glasses'?" A child psychiatrist once wanted me to remove a four-year-old child from our preschool because the psychiatrist thought her child would be "contaged" by another child's masturbating herself before nap time. She was shocked when I told her that some children go through this developmental stage, and that her child might too.

These forms of self-touch, or "touch therapy by another name" are important in their own right for health and well-being. Like diet and exercise, we need a daily dose of touch.

Infant Massage

Infant massage is practiced in most of the world. In many places, including Nigeria, Uganda, India, Bali, Fiji, New Guinea, New Zealand (the Maori), Venezuela, and Russia, infants are given a massage with oil after the daily bath and before sleeptime for the first several months of their lives.

Infant Massage in the Western World

Infant massage is only recently being discovered and researched in the Western world. Suddenly, in almost every city in the United States, there are massage therapy schools teaching parents how to massage their infants. The techniques they use are based on the teachings of two massage therapists who trained in India—Vimala Schneider McClure, who published books on infant massage in 1979 and again in 1989,[1] and Amelia Auckett, who published a book on infant massage in 1981.[2]

The Indian infant massage is a daily routine that begins in the first days of life. The infant is first laid on his or her stomach on the mother's outstretched legs, and each body part is individually stretched. Warm water and soap are applied to the legs, arms, and back, and then, as the infant is turned over, the abdomen, neck, and face. This massage looks like scrubbing clothes on an old washboard and it seems so extremely rigorous (almost rough) that I could not recommend it to parents. However, after the infants receive this massage and are swaddled, they sleep for prolonged periods (perhaps to recover from the stress of the massage). Also in its favor, some infant massage therapists attribute the precocious motor development of these infants to this daily massage. They suggest that the massage provides both relaxation and stimulation that helps circulation, digestion, elimination, and respiration.[3] They say that infants who are massaged sleep more soundly, that the massage relieves gas and colic, and that it helps the healing process if the infant is ill by easing his or her congestion and pain.[4]

Although infant massage training groups are now located in most parts of the United States, there has been very little research conducted on infant massage with healthy infants. Infant massage therapists say that massaging healthy infants helps the parent-infant bonding by promoting warm, positive relationships. It also reduces the infant's distress following painful procedures such as inoculations; it reduces pain from colic, constipation, and teething; it reduces sleep problems; and it makes the parents feel good while they are massaging their infants. The infant massage therapy groups also report that blind and deaf infants, those who are paralyzed, have cerebral palsy, or are premature, benefit from massages as well. Among other benefits, massaging seems to help infants become more aware of their bodies.

Massage Therapy with Infants Who Have Colic and Sleep Problems

Parents of infants who have colic and sleeping problems tell us our massage studies with their infants have saved their marriages, and saved their infants from abuse by helping them to calm their infants and get them to sleep. Others say it has gone too far when their seven-year-old child still needs a massage in order to go to sleep, as if it had become an addiction.

Massage Therapy with Premature Infants

Most of the data on the effects of infant massage come from studies on premature infants. During the last two decades, there have been a number of studies conducted, most of them technically labeled tactile/kinesthetic stimulation to avoid the negative connotations of the word massage.[5] The published results were generally positive. A recent global analysis of data from nineteen of these studies revealed that 72 percent of the massaged infants were positively affected.[6] Most of the infants experienced greater weight gain and better performance on developmental tasks. Those studies that did not report significant weight gain had used the wrong kind of touch, a light stroking procedure that babies do not like, probably because it feels like tickling. The babies who gained weight had been given deeper pressure massage, thus stimulating both tactile and pressure receptors (specialized nerve endings that respond to pressure).

One of the studies used in this global analysis was conducted in our lab (figure 7.1).[7] We gave massage therapy to premature newborns for ten days, forty-five minutes a day broken up into three fifteen-minute periods. The infants were all nine weeks premature, weighed about two pounds each, and had all been treated in intensive care for about three weeks before the study, which was started when they had graduated from the "Grower Nursery." At this time, the main focus was on weight gain. The massage therapy sessions were divided into three phases. For the first and last phase, the newborns were placed on their

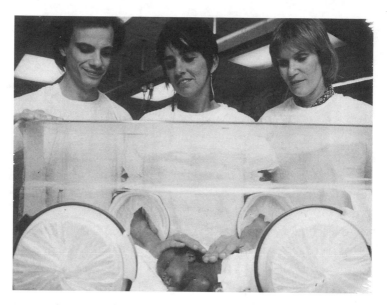

Figure 7.1
Preterm newborn being massaged in her incubator.

stomachs and gently stroked for five one-minute periods (twelve strokes at approximately five seconds per stroking motion) over each region in the following sequence: (1) from the top of the head to the neck, (2) from the neck across the shoulders, (3) from the upper back to the waist, (4) from the thigh to the foot to the thigh on both legs, and (5) from the shoulder to the hand to the shoulder on both arms. We used Swedish-type massage because, as already noted, infants prefer some degree of pressure. During the middle phase, we moved the infants' arms and legs back and forth in bicycling motions while the infants were lying on their backs.

The massaged infants in this study gained 47 percent more weight than those who were not massaged (even though both groups had the same amount of formula) (figure 7.2). They

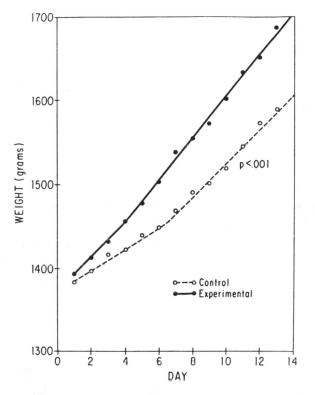

Figure 7.2
Daily weight gain in preterm newborns across a twelve-day period.

were awake and active more of the time, even though we had expected they would sleep more; they were more alert and responsive to the examiner's face and voice; and they showed more organized limb movements on a newborn test called the Brazelton scale. Finally, they were discharged from the hospital six days sooner than the others, a saving in hospital costs of approximately $3,000 per infant (the comparable cost savings today would be $10,000). If all the 470,000 premature infants born each year were massaged, that figure would translate into 4.7 billion dollars saved in hospital costs per year. Recently, we reduced the same study from ten days to five days and noted that there was still a 47 percent greater increase in weight gain in the premature babies who were massaged, suggesting that this would be even more cost-effective at the rate of five instead of ten days.[7]

This study was recently replicated by researchers in other parts of the world. In the Philippines, Dr. Cifra and her colleagues found exactly the same weight gain (47 percent) using exactly the same massage procedure with premature infants.[8] In Taiwan, another group of neonatologists, in addition to finding weight gain, also reported increased growth (length and head circumference) in their babies.[9] In Israel, the same procedure was used, but this time the massage therapists were the infants' mothers. In addition to weight gain, the authors of this study reported a decrease in postpartum depression in the mothers.[10]

In another study on massaging premature infants, thirty-three mother-infant pairs were randomly assigned to control, talking, or interactive groups.[11] In the interactive group, the infants received eye contact, massages, rocking, and talking. The treatments were given at specific times twenty-four hours after delivery. Before being discharged, the mothers and infants were observed during a feeding. The interactive group of infants was more responsive and easier to feed during their feeding interactions than either the control or talking groups.

In still another study, the biochemical and clinical responses of premature infants to massages were assessed.[12] The eleven infants in the study were born eleven weeks prematurely, weighed approximately two pounds, and were hospitalized for three days. For each, blood samples were obtained for stress-hormone (cortisol) levels forty-five minutes before the start of the massage and approximately one hour after the end of the massage. The cortisol levels consistently decreased after the massage.

Around the time we were conducting our studies on premature infants, our colleagues at Duke University Medical School were conducting similar studies, but on rat pups.[13] They removed rat pups from their mothers to explore touch deprivation. As mentioned earlier, the researchers stroked the depressed rat pups with a paintbrush, much like the mother rat would tongue-lick them, so the rat pups would grow normally. In several studies, the Duke team noted that the growth hormone decreased when the pups were removed from their mother. This decrease was noted in all the organs, including the heart, liver, and brain, but the levels returned to normal once the pups got stroked with the paint brush. The recent discovery of a growth gene that responds to touch suggests a strong genetic relationship between touching and growth.

This observation, plus the results of a study in Sweden, led us to some ideas about how to explain the touch/weight-gain relationship.[14] The Swedish study reported that stimulating the mouth of the newborn (and the breast of the breastfeeding mother) led to an increase in the food-absorption hormones gastrin and insulin. The study further suggested that massage therapy on other parts of the body might also lead to an increase in food-absorption hormones. As this increase could itself explain the weight gain, we began measuring these hormones (glucose and insulin), and found that the massaged infants have higher insulin levels. Unfortunately, the downside is that breastfeeding mothers (who do not want to gain weight) might also gain weight for the same reason.

Massaging Cocaine-Exposed Premature Infants

We also massaged cocaine-exposed premature infants, hoping that they too would benefit from massage therapy.[15] We used the same type of massage described above three times daily for a ten-day period. After our treatment, the massaged, cocaine-exposed premature infants had fewer medical complications and less irritability; they had a 28 percent greater daily weight gain than similar infants who were not massaged, and they showed more mature motor activity. These results are very encouraging for crack- and cocaine-addicted babies, who have such a hard time getting a foothold on life.

Massaging HIV-Exposed Neonates

The AIDS epidemic has led to increasing numbers of babies who were exposed to HIV prenatally. To determine whether massage therapy helped their mental, motor, and social development, we conducted a study where we taught the mothers how to massage their infants.[16] We had almost 100 percent cooperation from the mothers, an unusually high rate that might have resulted from the mothers' feelings of guilt for exposing their infants to HIV. After two weeks of massage therapy, these infants showed greater weight gain, better performance on the social and motor items of a newborn test, and fewer stress behaviors than the control infants.

Massaging Pregnant Women to Prevent Premature Births

Optimally, massage could decrease the rate of premature deliveries. In a recent publication, we reported that massage therapy decreased stress hormones and lowered the prematurity rate.[17]

Motor-Impaired Infants

In a study conducted by researchers R. Hansen and G. Ulrey, nine handicapped infants performed such activities as reaching for objects and manipulating them; ten handicapped infants performed these activities, plus they received massages from their mothers.[18] The mothers in the activities *plus* massages group showed more attachment to their infants, and the infants themselves benefited by performing their activities better.

Depressed Mothers Massaging Their Infants

We are now routinely teaching parents to provide the massages because it allows the infants daily massages at no cost, and the parents might also benefit from the act of giving the massages. For example, we taught depressed mothers to massage their infants in order to help decrease the mothers' depression and help reduce the infants' distress behavior and disturbed sleep patterns.[19] For this study we asked the infants' mothers to perform a fifteen-minute massage daily for a two-week period. After two weeks, the infants were able to fall asleep faster, they slept longer and were less fussy, and the mothers played more easily with them. The decreased fussiness and the improved sleep suggested to us that massage therapy might help infants who have colic, or infants who have difficulty sleeping, so we are now doing studies with those infants.

Fathers as Massage Therapists

During a film we made for Australian television, we demonstrated infant massage to fathers. The film's producer felt it was important to get the fathers more involved in caregiving because, he told us, "fathers in Australia spend very little time with their infants."

Since that demonstration, there has been a study on Australian fathers massaging their infants.[20] In the study, Australian fathers with first-born babies were given a one-month training program in baby massage, including a bathing massage technique. At a three-month home observation, the fathers showed greater involvement with their infants, and the infants greeted their fathers with more eye contact, more smiling, vocalizing, and reaching responses, and less avoidance behavior than they had previously shown (figure 7.3). We subsequently conducted a similar study with a group of first-time American fathers, and these fathers too became more interactive with their infants after massaging the infants for a month.[21]

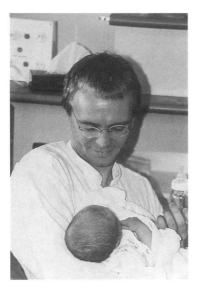

Figure 7.3
Fathers caring for infants.

Grandparent Volunteers as Massage Therapists

One of the greatest deterrents to delivering massage to preterm infants is the cost of providing the massage. We have found that, as mentioned earlier, teaching "grandparent" volunteers is a no-cost way to deliver massage therapy. In a study designed to measure massage therapy effects on sexually and physically abused infants and the benefits for the volunteer grandparents who are giving the massage, we had the grandparent volunteers massage neglected and abused children in a shelter.[22] (These volunteers were not really the grandparents of the infants, but they preferred that term over "elderly.") Some older people experience failure to thrive because of touch deprivation, just as some infants do,[23] so this is therapy for them, too. A recent survey indicates that failure to thrive and depression are fairly common among older people (between 5 and 26 percent).[24] Symptoms, similar to those in younger people,[25] include complaints of physical problems, feelings of hopelessness and worthlessness, memory impairments, negative mood states, and poor concentration.[26] In addition, there can be frequent night wakings, increased stress hormone levels, and problems with the immune system.[25] This can lead to failure to thrive, with decreased appetite and weight loss, and a diminished state of health overall. For all these symptoms of depression in older people, pet therapy (having and holding pets) has been effective,[27] but massage therapy seems to help even more, especially when the elderly are the ones giving the massages.

In our study, the grandparent volunteers reported fewer depressive symptoms, an improved mood, and lower anxiety levels after both giving and receiving a massage; plus, their stress hormone levels decreased. After a month of giving or getting the therapy, their lifestyles improved, including more social contacts, fewer trips to the doctor's office, and fewer cups of coffee. These changes probably also helped to improve their sleep and their self-esteem. Somewhat surprisingly, the improvements were greater after a month of giving infants the massages than they were after a month of receiving their own massages.

This study shows that massage therapy is not only effective for infants, but also helps the adults who are massaging them. The massages are free, and everyone seems to benefit. See box 7.1.

Box 7.1
Infant Massage Instructions

> The massage procedure for older infants (three to twenty-four months) is a little more complex and a little more interesting than the procedure for young infants (birth to three months) described earlier in this chapter. Because older infants like more variety, this massage uses more varied techniques (figure 7.4). It lasts approximately fifteen minutes, as follows:
>
> *Start with the infant face up*
> 1. *Face*: Strong stroking motions along both sides of the face.
>
> 2. *Legs*: Apply oil with gentle strokes from hip to foot. Use long milking strokes toward the ankle with your hand wrapped around the leg. Squeeze and twist your hands as if you were wringing out wet clothes—from foot to hip. Massage the foot, using a thumb-over-thumb motion covering the entire bottom of the foot. Squeeze each toe gently and finish with a soothing pull. Press your thumbs into the bottom of the baby's foot. Make small circles all over the top of the ankle and foot. Make long milking strokes with your hands wrapped around the baby's leg, going toward the heart and then back to the ankle. Roll the baby's leg in between your hands from knee to ankle. Use long gentle strokes toward the ankle. Repeat these movements on the other leg.
>
> *Continued*

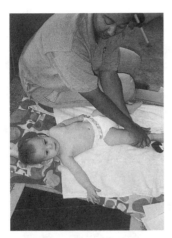

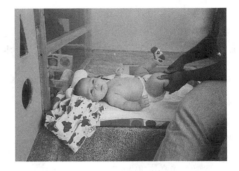

Figure 7.4
Some examples of infant massage techniques.

3. *Stomach*: Hand over hand in paddlewheel fashion, go higher to lower on the stomach. Make a circular motion with your fingers, going in a clockwise direction from the appendix. Gently feel for gas bubbles and work them out in a clockwise direction.

4. *Chest*: Make strokes on both sides of the baby's chest with the flats of your fingers, going from the middle to the outside. Use cross strokes, starting from the center of the chest and going over the shoulders. Make strokes on both sides of the chest simultaneously, with the flats of your hands going over the chest to the shoulders.

5. *Arms*: With long gentle strokes, apply oil from the shoulders to the hands. Use the same procedure as for the legs.

6. *Face*: Make strokes along both sides of the face. Use the flats of your fingers across the forehead. Make circular strokes over the temples and the hinge of the jaw. Use the flats of your fingers over the baby's nose, cheeks, jaw, and chin. Lightly massage the area behind the ears and continue the circular movements to the rest of the scalp.

Turn the baby face down
1. *Back*: Gently apply oil in long downward strokes. Move your hands from side to side to caress the infant's back, including the sides. Go hand over hand from the upper back to the buttocks with the flats of your hands contoured to the shape of the back. Make gentle strokes along the length of the back down to the bottom of the feet. Make a circular motion with your fingertips, from the head to the buttocks over the long muscles on each side of the spine. Do not rub over the spine. Lightly massage the baby's neck and shoulders, using soothing circular strokes.

These massages have many benefits, both for the babies being massaged and for the caregivers doing the massaging, and should be included in the daily routine of all infants and developing babies.

8

Massage Therapy for Children, Adolescents, and Adults

The *Ayurveda*, the earliest known medical text from India (around 1800 B.C.), lists massages, along with diet and exercise, as primary healing practices of that time. As Jules Older notes, even the English word *shampoo*, which usually involves a head massage, comes from the ancient Hindi word *champna*, meaning to "press."[1] Over the course of history, massage therapy has been used for many conditions, from labor pains to mental illness, restoring movement in fractured, strained, or wounded limbs, and for rheumatic diseases, stimulating the breast for milk, stomach pains, and aging.

Massage improves circulation, helps eliminate waste, reduces swelling, and soothes the peripheral and central nervous system. Its other uses include treating pressure sores in bedridden patients, massaging the gums for gum disease, and massaging the prostate for the treatment of prostatitis. The only conditions that have been listed as potential contraindications are bursitis (inflammation in the joints), cellulitis (inflammation in the legs), inflammation due to infection, and severe varicose veins. Some physicians also warn that the neck can be a dangerous area to massage, but these contraindications are purely speculative and not based on any research data.

Jules Older comments on the very exotic uses of massage in different cultures. He notes that in New Zealand, Maori mothers massage their children's noses to improve their shape, and they massage their legs to lengthen and straighten them.[2] In Cuba, a garlic and oil massage is applied to the stomach following "a meal lodged in the stomach where it caused pain and fever."[3] In Samoa, massages are used for every disorder from migraine to diarrhea. There they use a mixture of coconut milk, flowers from trees and plants, and roots of grasses for their massaging.[3]

In the field of touch, massage therapy has received the lion's share of attention. This is probably because it is one of the most popular of the touch therapies and lends itself to many more conditions than, for example, chiropractic care, which focuses primarily on the back. In addition, healthy people are more likely to use it as a preventive measure to reduce stress. Finally, it is one of the oldest touch therapies. Of all the massage therapies, Swedish massage is the most popularly used, probably because it is one of the easiest to perform.

The medical community is gradually accepting massage therapy. Although touch therapies were the foundation of medicine in the West from the time of Hippocrates (400 B.C.), they were replaced by drugs after the advent of pharmaceuticals in the 1940s. Until the early 1950s, most patients received a massage—at least a backrub—on a daily basis in the hospital. Then massages unfortunately became associated with massage parlors instead of hospital therapies, but over the past few years, the increasing amount of research data on the positive effects of massage therapy has led to its increasing popularity as both a profession and a legitimate therapy. Physicians are beginning to prescribe massages for such painful conditions as arthritis, lower back pain, and migraine headaches *before* prescribing drugs or surgery, to determine whether this less invasive therapy with no negative side effects can help a particular condition.

Unfortunately, the United States is a "Johnny come lately" in this field and does not yet have the widespread insurance coverage for massage therapy that other countries such as England or Germany have, partly because, although there are many studies on the benefits of massage for infants and children, most of the research information on adults in massage therapy comes from anecdotal case studies. In those studies, the effects could be considered merely placebo effects because the adults are receiving additional attention and have certain expectations about being treated. Studies of this kind are not accepted in the orthodox scientific and medical community without sham control groups (a sham massage group would receive no pressure, for example), attention control groups (they receive some attention but no massage therapy), or treatment comparison groups (they receive another form of therapy, such as relaxation therapy). The following are brief summaries of studies on massage therapy with children and adults that did have appropriate attention control or treatment comparison groups.

Facilitating Alertness

Enhancing EEG Pattern of Alertness
In this job-stress study, the staff and faculty of a medical school were massaged in massage chairs in their offices for fifteen minutes a day during their lunch periods.[4] These massage sessions, which took place over a one-month period, involved deep pressure in the back, shoulders, neck, and head regions. Although we thought that these people might be even sleepier than usual after their midday massage, they reported instead that they experienced heightened alertness, much like a runner's high. This led us to record their electroencephalogram (EEG) patterns before, during, and after the massage sessions.

When you are going to sleep, your alpha levels normally increase, but here they decreased. This decrease, combined with increased theta and decreased beta waves, suggested a pattern of heightened alertness. We then asked these participants to do math computations in order to determine whether this EEG pattern of heightened alertness would be translated into performance. The time they took to do their computations was significantly reduced, and the accuracy of the computations was increased following the massages, suggesting that the fifteen-minute massages had, in fact, enhanced their alertness and cognitive performance. Everyone should tell their bosses how much a fifteen-minute massage can help to reduce their job stress and improve their performance, so massage breaks can become as routine as coffee breaks.

Attention Deficits
Autism   Children with autism are often described as extremely sensitive to touch; they often dislike being touched. In spite of this, however, we have noted that they love being massaged, maybe because, unlike random touching in social situations, massaging is predictable. In our first study on preschool children with autism, their disruptive behavior in the classroom decreased, and their ability to relate to their teachers increased following a ten-day period of massage.[5] In our second study, parents massaged their children with autism every night.[6] The children experienced the same benefits as in the first study, but their sleep also improved. Massaging and giving backrubs is an easy therapy for teachers and parents to learn, and it should also make parents and teachers feel better, because children with autism do not usually like being touched, which can leave their parents and teachers feeling frustrated that their affection is being rejected. Massaging the children is therefore an important way they can share affectionate touch with these children,

Figure 8.1
A young child massaging her massage therapist friend in a massage chair.

and we should encourage its use in reaching out to them (figure 8.1).

Attention Deficit Hyperactivity Disorder In a similar study, ADHD adolescents were given massage therapy or relaxation therapy (the control group) thirty minutes a day for ten consecutive school days.[7] The massage therapy group versus the relaxation therapy group rated themselves as "happier," and observers rated them as less fidgety following the sessions.

After the two-week period, their teachers (who did not know which children were getting which therapy) reported that the students who turned out to be the massaged ones spent more time on their work and were rated lower on the hyperactivity/behavior problem scale, based on their classroom behavior.

Alleviating Depression and Anxiety

Abused and Neglected Children

Depression and anxiety are big problems for abused and neglected children. In a study we conducted, staff members and volunteers in a shelter gave a fifteen-minute massage every day for a month to a group of sexually and physically abused children.[8] This group was compared to one who heard Dr. Seuss stories. After one month of the massage therapy, the children's sleep increased and they became more alert and less depressed. The caregivers also reported that the children became more active and sociable. The group who had the stories read to them did not show as much improvement.

Posttraumatic Stress Disorder

Many children experienced posttraumatic stress symptoms following Hurricane Andrew, which devastated the Miami area in 1995.[9] A group of these children were given massage therapy twice a week for a month. In a comparison between the massage therapy group and a control group who watched a relaxing video, the PTSD symptoms and depression decreased in those receiving the massage therapy, but not in those watching videos. Anxiety also decreased in the massaged group, as did their problems indicated by their drawings. On the first day of the massage therapy, for example, a girl drew herself as a very small, dark-colored figure who had no facial features.

On the last day of the massages, though, she drew a birthday party with balloons, sunshine, and birds, and friends attending her birthday party. These gratifying results suggest that massage therapists should not only massage the adults and search dogs, as they did following Hurricane Andrew, but also the children. At stressful times like this, children may receive less than their normal amount of physical affection from their parents and teachers; massages seem to help that problem a great deal.

Child and Adolescent Psychiatric Patients

Child and adolescent psychiatric patients are usually both extremely depressed and very anxious; these problems get in the way of their treatment. In a study on hospitalized depressed children and adolescents,[10] we gave them back massages for a week and compared them with a control group who viewed relaxing videotapes. After one week, the massaged children and adolescents were less depressed and less anxious, they had lower stress-hormones levels (saliva cortisol levels, as well as lower urinary cortisol and norepinephrine levels). The videotapes made of their sleep behavior revealed more organized sleep patterns. In addition, nurses on the unit rated the massaged group as less anxious and more cooperative than the control group by the last day of the study.

Bulimia and Anorexia in Adolescent Girls

Adolescents with bulimia (overeating and then vomiting) also experience severe depression (which may in fact be a large reason for their problem). Following a month of massages, adolescents with bulimia had fewer symptoms of depression, lower anxiety levels, and lower stress hormones (urinary cortisol levels).[11] Their eating habits also improved in the short run and they had a less distorted body image.

Chronic Fatigue

Although some physicians have recently speculated that chronic fatigue may be an immune disease, people with chronic fatigue syndrome also tend to have high scores on depression scales. In a recent study, we compared people with chronic fatigue syndrome who were receiving massage therapy with those who were only receiving sham TENS (transcutaneous electrical stimulation that is not turned on, a placebo).[12] In contrast to the sham TENS group, immediately after the massage therapy, on the first and last days of the study, the massage therapy group had lower depression and anxiety scores, and lower stress hormones (salivary cortisol levels). The longer term effects (last day versus first day) showed that the massage therapy group also had fewer symptoms of physical distress, less depression, lower stress-hormone levels (urinary cortisol), more hours of sleep, and higher urinary dopamine levels (dopamine usually has an antidepressant effect) than the sham TENS group.

Alcohol/Drug Addiction

Certainly, addicted people have a problem with depression and anxiety. Paradoxically, although the addictions often start as a way of trying to lessen the effects of depression, the use of alcohol and drugs typically ends up worsening the depression. Because of the difficulty in finding a suitable control group or comparison treatment, we have not yet been able to try massage therapy for addiction, but another research group did a study where massage therapy was given to both the addicted people and their counselors in chemical-dependency treatment programs, as well as to those recovering after treatment.[13] Although that study did not have a suitable control group either, several benefits were noted, including deeper relaxation, less depression, greater self-acceptance, and quicker detoxification.

We conducted a self-massage study for smokers with similar success,[14] teaching the women how to massage their earlobes and the men how to massage their hands (they found massaging their earlobes embarrassing). We instructed them to use this self-massage every time they had an urge for a cigarette, and in doing so, the number of cigarettes they smoked per day decreased. Twenty-seven percent of the subjects stopped smoking entirely.

Grandparent Volunteers Massaging Infants

Older people also suffer from depression, which may relate in part to touch deprivation. In the course of using volunteer "grandparents" to massage abused infants,[15] we were surprised to find how much the grandparents themselves benefited from giving these massages. Following a one-month period of massaging the infants, their depression decreased and they experienced increased self-esteem and decreased cortisol levels. We then compared grandparent volunteers giving versus receiving massages themselves. They first massaged the infants for a month, and then received massages for a month. As previously noted in chapters 2 and 7, these grandparent volunteers benefited more from giving the massages than from receiving the massages. Their emotional states and their self-esteem improved, as did their lifestyle habits, including drinking fewer cups of coffee per day, making more social phone calls, and taking fewer trips to the doctor's office. One of the reasons they may have done better giving than receiving massages is that they reported feeling awkward about being touched. They said they had never been touched the way they were when they were massaged. Also, giving the massages may have made them feel more useful and valuable because they were able to help the infants.

Potential for Massage Therapy Decreasing Depression

In all the above studies, depression and anxiety levels decreased, and the stress hormones (norepinephrine, epinephrine, cortisol) were reduced. This could be explained by the shift in brain waves we have noted in our studies, with the EEG showing a shift from right frontal activity (typically seen in depressed people) to left frontal activity (typically seen in happy people)[16] following a massage. These shifts were accompanied by an increase in positive mood. In our study on depressed adolescent mothers and their infants, their right frontal EEG activity shifted in the direction of left frontal EEG activity following a twenty-minute massage.[16] These electrophysiological changes (from a negative to a positive EEG pattern) and the related chemical changes (the stress hormones decreasing) may be what lies behind the decrease in depression that is noted following massage therapy. Additionally, the beneficial neurotransmitters serotonin and dopamine, both of which increase with antidepressants, also increased following massage therapy, which could further explain these findings.

Reducing Acute Pain during Painful Events and Procedures

Childbirth Labor

In many countries such as India, pregnant women are massaged several times daily for relaxation and to reduce their anxiety levels. This therapy is beneficial for both the pregnant woman and her fetus. In our Touch Research Institutes, we have been teaching the partners of pregnant women to massage the women during pregnancy and labor.[17] Ultrasound images taken during the massages reveal some very happy responses from the fetus. Most of them seem to like the massage, as can be seen by their "smiles" (relaxed faces) on the ultrasound. When we coded fetal movements after the massages, we found that their activity level normalized—they were neither too active nor too inactive as judged by the ultrasonographer. This may be due to the reduced anxiety and depression in the mothers following the massages. In addition, we found that the labors were shorter for these mothers than they were for the mothers doing breathing exercises alone (the control group), and the need for medications or cesarean sections was decreased, reducing hospital costs significantly. Finally, in a newborn examination, those newborns whose mothers were massaged performed better on self-consoling behavior and on responses to faces and sounds than the newborns in the control group. An important side effect was that the anxiety of the partners participating in the labors was also reduced just by giving the massages. Some women in our study who were allergic to medication even had their doctors prescribing the massage therapy as their medication of choice for pain. Because this therapy has so many benefits and incurs no costs, delivery units everywhere should certainly adopt it.

Massage Therapy Prior to Debridement for Burn Patients
Debridement (skin brushing) following severe burns is among the most painful medical procedures one can experience. Anticipatory anxiety tends to run high, but massage therapy can reduce this anxiety prior to debridement, and can indirectly alleviate the pain during the procedure (figure 8.2). Following thirty-minute massage treatments for five days prior to debridement, burn patients were found to have lower anxiety and an associated decrease in stress hormones.[18] Pain was also significantly decreased over the five days of the study, as was depression, probably due to the decrease in pain. We found similar

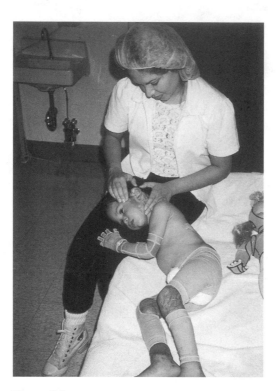

Figure 8.2
Burned child being massaged on nonburned parts by mother.

results with children in a second study.[19] In a third, we are massaging postburn people after they are out of the hospital and in the healing process, which involves not only some residual pain, but also a lot of itching. We found that massaging their burn wounds regularly with cocoa butter helps to decrease both their pain and their itching.[20]

Postoperative Pain
Surgeons need to be aware of how useful massage therapy can be for their patients recovering from surgery. In a study on

postoperative pain in 116 patients who underwent thoracic surgery,[21] the patients assessed their pain before and after massage by marking it on a scale from 1 to 10. After being massaged, their pain level significantly decreased. Unfortunately, like many other massage therapy studies of this kind, there was no control group, so the standard orthodox medical opinion could be that these decreases were only a response to receiving the additional attention. However, those of us who have studied and worked in the field know better.

Reducing Pain in Chronic Pain Conditions

Juvenile Rheumatoid Arthritis
Children with juvenile rheumatoid arthritis experience chronic pain because the anti-inflammatory drugs used for their pain are only partially effective, and other drugs such as narcotics cannot be used because of their potentially addictive effects. For this reason, other pain-relieving therapies such as massage therapy are being explored with these children. In a one-month study in which parents gave daily massages to their juvenile-rheumatoid-arthritis children, there were several positive effects noted.[22] After massage therapy (compared to the progressive muscle relaxation therapy received by the control group), the massaged children had decreased anxiety and stress levels (cortisol) after the first and last sessions, and decreased pain over the one-month period. One possible explanation for the decreased pain is that the pressure nerves stimulated during a massage transmit their message to the brain faster because they are longer fibers; then the gate is shut to the pain signal, which is transmitted on shorter fibers.[23] Another possibility is increased serotonin production. Moderate increases in serotonin levels have been reported after massage therapy for

other conditions; the same thing could be happening with these children.[24]

Fibromyalgia

In a study on fibromyalgia, people with this syndrome were randomly assigned to either a massage therapy group, a transcutaneous electrical stimulation (TENS) group, or a group that supposedly received transcutaneous electrical stimulation, but the machine was not plugged in (sham TENS). (Transcutaneous stimulation is a light electrical current transmitted through a small metal rod and rolled across the same body parts that were massaged in the massage group.) The treatments were thirty-minute sessions twice a week for five weeks.[25] The massage therapy group (versus the TENS and sham TENS groups) reported lower anxiety and depression, and their stress-hormone levels were lower immediately after the therapy sessions on the first and last days of the study. The TENS group showed similar changes, but only after therapy on the last day of the study. The massage therapy group additionally reported less pain, less stiffness and fatigue, and fewer nights of difficult sleep.

Headaches

Twenty-one women with chronic tension headaches received ten sessions of upper body massage (not including the head) consisting of deep pressure techniques, in addition to softer massage techniques that were used at the beginning of the session.[26] Their trigger points (knots in the muscles) were carefully but forcefully massaged. At the end of the study, the range of their neck movement had increased, and the number of days they had headaches had decreased. The women were also less depressed after the treatment period. Again, this study did not have a control group, but our study on migraine headaches had already shown that the massaged group had significantly fewer migraines than the relaxation control group.[24] This migraine headache study had a very serendipitous beginning. A surgeon at the University of Maryland Medical School mistakenly cut a tendon at the base of a patient's skull, after which her migraine headaches miraculously disappeared. Our massage study with migraine patients focused on the area of that tendon and was extremely successful, including a significant increase in serotonin levels and the number of headache-free days.

Lower Back Pain

In another chronic pain study conducted by our Touch Research Institutes, we used massage therapy on a group with lower back pain.[27] By the end of the study, the lower back pain in the massage group was reduced. In addition, they showed improvement on range-of-motion tests and also had higher serotonin and dopamine levels.

Cancer Pain

This study, by another group, compared different procedures for coping with cancer pain, including distraction, relaxation, and massage,[28] all of which turned out to be effective in pain management, perceived ability to decrease pain, and pain intensity ratings measured before and after the therapies. The massage therapy, however, was the most effective.

General Pain

Massage therapy is usually given by another person, but in this study a touch device called the Dermapoints Massageroller was used as a self-massager.[29] It is a steel hand-held rod with wheels of small, pointed steel triangles that move across the skin as you roll it, much like a miniature rolling pin for dough, but with points. The Massageroller both increased skin temperature (suggesting enhanced blood circulation) and decreased muscle tension.

In another study, a therapist gave connective-tissue massage to relieve general pain.[30] Beta endorphins (brain neurotransmitters associated with pain relief) were measured in the blood of the twelve volunteers before and after one thirty-minute session of connective-tissue massage. After the massage, there was a moderate increase in beta-endorphin levels, lasting for about one hour, which was linked with pain relief and a feeling of well-being after the treatment.

Theories about Why These Therapies Work

Gate Theory
Pain alleviation has most frequently been attributed to the gate theory.[31] This theory, previously discussed in section on juvenile rheumatoid arthritis and in chapter 5, suggests that pressure or cold temperature can alleviate pain because the nerve fibers in the skin that sense pain are shorter and less insulated than the nerve fibers for pressure and cold temperature. The brain receives the pressure or cold-temperature stimuli before the pain stimulus and, so to speak, closes the gate to any further stimulation, so the brain never receives the pain stimulus.

Sleep Deficits
Another theory involving pain alleviation by massage therapy has to do with the effects of being deprived of deep or restorative sleep. During quiet sleep, the brain normally releases growth hormone. When there is less deep sleep, this chemical is absent and pain is experienced. Also, when there is less deep sleep, another chemical called substance P is released,

which is notable for causing pain. Deep sleep is needed both to allow release of growth hormone and avoid release of substance P. One of the leading theories for the pain associated with fibromyalgia syndrome, for example, is that substance P is released because the patient is deep-sleep-deprived.[32] It is interesting to note that those in our fibromyalgia syndrome study who had massage therapy experienced more quiet/deep sleep and less pain following the treatment period.[32]

Reducing Neuromuscular Problems

Down's Syndrome
In a recent study, we found that Down's syndrome children had improved motor function and muscle tone following massage therapy.[33] In addition, their muscle tone improved, so they had less hypotonicity, and they were able to perform better on fine and gross motor assessments.

Cerebral Palsy
In this study, we were concerned with reducing the children's spastic movements so they could have more control over their motor activities.[34] Following one month of massage, they were less spastic and their hypertonicity had decreased. In addition, their performance on motor assessments improved.

Multiple Sclerosis
After a month of massages given for thirty minutes twice a week, women with multiple sclerosis improved their functional activity and marginally improved their ability to get around, and as a result were probably less depressed.[35] In addition, their handgrip strength increased, which probably contributed to their improvement in daily activities.

Spinal Cord Injury

Massage therapy had similarly positive effects on a group of adults with spinal cord injuries.[36] Following five weeks of twice weekly massages, their functional activity improved, and they experienced an increased range of motion in their wrists and elbows.

Autoimmune Disorders

Asthma in Children

Asthma is considered an autoimmune disorder, in which the body fights its own immune system. Anticipating asthma attacks is thought to make children very anxious, and this anxiety in turn makes the asthma condition worse. Because of our studies on other clinical conditions that showed lower anxiety levels after massage therapy, we tried this with asthmatic children. Twenty-minute bedtime massages were given to them daily for a month by their parents.[37] Immediately after the massages the parents' anxiety decreased, the children's self-reported anxiety levels decreased, their mood improved, and their stress hormones (cortisol levels) decreased. Most importantly, over the one-month period, the children had significantly fewer asthma attacks and they showed significantly improved pulmonary functions, including improved peak airflow, which measures how efficiently you can fill and empty your lungs.

Diabetes in Children

Juvenile diabetes (type I) is another autoimmune disease. In this case, the pancreas does not produce enough insulin naturally to keep the body's glucose levels normal. As with asthma, this is a stressful disease for both the children and their parents, because the parents' involvement in their children's treatment can be a negative experience; for example, having to monitor dietary compliance, take blood samples, and give their children insulin shots are all stressful and unpleasant tasks. We expected that giving parents a more positive role in their children's treatment by having them massage the children daily before bedtime might improve their experience,[38] and we were right. The parents' anxiety and depressed mood levels were lower, and their children's anxiety levels and depressed mood levels were also lower immediately following the massage therapy sessions. At the end of the one-month period of our study, the parents reported that their children's insulin and food regulation scores had improved, and their blood glucose levels had decreased from very high average levels into the normal range (from 158 to 118).

Dermatitis in Children
Children with eczema are often depressed by their skin condition. Having parents massage them as they apply their medication cream improved their condition, reducing the redness, scaling, and itching.[39]

Immune Disorders

Healthy College Students
In an immune study, fifty healthy college students were assigned to one of a number of relaxation methods—lying quietly with eyes closed, massage therapy, progressive muscle relaxation (tightening and relaxing muscles sequentially throughout the body), visual imagery, or a control group.[40] Immune responses (immunoglobulin A) and stress hormone levels (cortisol) were measured from saliva samples taken before and after the twenty-minute sessions. Of all the different groups, the students in the massage group showed the

largest increase in salivary immunoglobulin concentrations, followed by the progressive muscle relaxation and visual imagery groups. This shows that massages are highly beneficial to the immune system.

Cancer

A pilot study was conducted to examine the effects of gentle back massage on the well-being of women receiving radiation treatments for breast cancer.[41] In this study, the women were their own controls, using pre- and postmassage measures for the comparison following the back massage therapy. These women reported less distress, greater tranquility and vitality, and less tension and tiredness.

In another study we recently conducted, we were able to show an increase in natural killer cells after one month of massage therapy.[42] This probably contributed to a slower progression of the disease, as natural killer cells ward off cancer cells.

Yet another study focused on scar formation following breast cancer surgery (which may disrupt the normal breast contour) and found that frequently massaging the scar reduced scar formation.[43] Unfortunately, because most states do not allow anyone but an obstetrician/gynecologist to touch a woman's breasts, this study will be difficult to replicate. After breast surgery, many women do not enjoy massaging themselves or having their partners massage them, so these factors combine to make it difficult to assess the effects of massage on breast-scar reduction.

HIV-Positive Adults and Adolescents

In a study on HIV-positive adults, natural killer cells (the immune cells that are on the front line of the immune system) increased following twenty days of massage.[44] In this study, twenty-nine gay men (twenty HIV-positive, nine HIV-negative) were massaged for one month, then not massaged the next month. Comparisons made between the on and off months showed that during the massage months the natural killer cells increased, but there was no increase in the cells (CD4 cells) that are normally killed by the HIV virus, possibly because the HIV men were already severely immune-compromised. Stress hormones (cortisol levels) also decreased. We know that stress hormones kill immune cells, including natural killer cells, so the increase in natural killer cells associated with massage therapy was probably related to the decrease in these stress hormones following the massage therapy. Because natural killer cells are the front line of defense in the immune system, and because they combat the growth and proliferation of viral and cancer cells, the HIV patients who received the massage therapy might have experienced fewer infections such as pneumonia and other viruses that often are fatal to them. In a subsequent study with HIV adolescents who were less immune-compromised, we were able to show an increase in the CD4 cells.[45] This suggested that we were slowing down the disease process itself by the massage therapy.

Summary

Each of these conditions seems to have benefited from massage therapy treatments. Unique changes, such as increased peak air flow in asthma or decreased glucose levels in diabetes, occurred in each study. In addition, there were common findings noted across most of the studies, including decreased anxiety, depression, and stress hormones (cortisol). Physiological arousal and stress hormones appear to be lowered by the pressure stimulation associated with massage. Decreased stress hormones would lead to enhanced immune function because cortisol kills immune cells. We have come to realize that pressure is critical. Light stroking is generally disliked because it feels like a tickle.

Although other findings were unique to specific studies because they were the only studies that measured them—for example our study on enhanced alertness and math performance along with the EEG pattern of heightened alertness—we can safely suggest that all recipients of massage would probably experience these benefits. These changes may be related to increased vagal activity by stimulating the vagus nerve (one of the twelve nerves in the brain), which enhances relaxation, reduces stress hormones, slows down the heart rate, and increases alertness. As vagal activity slows the nervous system down to a more alert, relaxed state, people not only feel better, but they also perform better, are able to sleep better, and are less likely to get sick. This happens because of the diminished stress hormones and the resulting enhanced immune function.

Other results may be specific to the condition, and we probably would not generalize from them. For example, the premature infant needs to gain weight, whereas a full-term newborn does not, and a postpartum mother would certainly not want to gain weight from being massaged. In the premature infant, an increase in vagal activity accompanying the massage increases food-absorption hormones like glucose levels (a branch of the vagus nerve stimulates this release of food-absorption hormones in the gastrointestinal tract), so the premature infant can gain weight because of the increased food absorption. This does not seem to apply to full-term newborns, probably because they are already at an optimal weight. In another example, the person with asthma needs to breathe better, and a side effect of the massage therapy is better breathing, probably again because of increased vagal nerve activity and its calming of the central nervous system. In all of these massage therapy studies, we have hoped to specifically alter the disease condition.

Conclusion

The Touch Research Institutes have other ongoing projects, using touch therapy with cancer, comas, and muscular dystrophy in children, acne in adolescents, and carpal tunnel syndrome and psoriasis in adults. We hope to see similar positive results, because many of us have at least one of these conditions and because all of us would feel better with a little less stress. As it has been in countless cultures throughout the centuries, massage therapy should probably be right up there at the top of the health priority list, along with diet and exercise. After all, everyone loves a little touch therapy.

Notes

Preface

1. Anderson, G. C. (1995). Touch and the kangaroo care method. In Field, T. M. (ed.), *Touch in Early Development*. Mahwah, N.J.: Lawrence Erlbaum Associates Inc., 35–51.

2. Field, T. M., Ignatoff, E., Stringer, S., Brennan, J., Greenberg, R., Widmayer, S., and Anderson, G. (1982). Nonnutritive sucking during tube feedings: Effects on preterm neonates in an Intensive Care Unit. *Pediatrics* 70 (3): 381–384.

3. Field, T. M., Schanberg, S., Scafidi, F., Bower, C., Vega Lahr, N., Garcia, R., Nystrom, J., and Kuhn, C. (1986). Tactile/kinesthetic stimulation effects on preterm neonates. *Pediatrics* 77 (5): 654–658.

4. Schanberg, S. (1995). Genetic basis for touch effects. In Field, T. M. (ed.), *Touch in Early Development*. Mahwah, N.J.: Lawrence Erlbaum Associates, 211–229.

5. Field, T. M., Harding, J., Soliday, B., Lasko, D., Gonzalez, N., and Valdeon, C. (1994). Touching in infant, toddler and preschool nurseries. *Early Child Development and Care* 98: 113–120.

Chapter 1

1. Settle, F. (1991). My experience in a Romanian orphanage. *Massage Therapy Journal* (Fall): 64–72.

2. Field, T. M., Harding, J., Soliday, B., Lasko, D., Gonzalez, N., and Valdeon, C. (1994). Touching in infant, toddler and preschool nurseries. *Early Child Development and Care* 98: 113–120.

3. Montagu, A. (1986). *Touching: The Human Significance of the Skin*. New York: Harper & Row, 270.

4. Bloch, H. (2000). Learning by mouth in the first months of life. Paper presented at the International Conference on Infant Studies, Brighton, England.

5. Field, T. M., and Howell, S. (1992). Touching teaches, nurtures children. *Parents' News* 17: 20.

6. Henley, N. M. (1973). The politics of touch. In Brown, P. (ed.), *Radical Psychology*. New York: Colophon Books, 420–433.

7. Jorgenson, J. (1996). Therapeutic use of companion animals in health care. *Journal of Nursing Scholarship* 29: 249–254.

8. Schanberg, S., and Field, T. M. (1987). Sensory deprivation stress and supplemental stimulation in the rat pup and preterm human neonate. *Child Development* 58: 1431–1447.

9. Tronick, E., Morelli, G. A., and Winn, S. (1987). Multiple caretaking of Efe (pygmy) infants. *American Anthropologist* 89: 96–106.

10. Jourard, S. M. (1966). An exploratory study of body accessibility. *British Journal of Social and Clinical Psychology* 5: 221–231.

11. Field, T. M. (1999). Preschoolers in America are touched less and are more aggressive than preschoolers in France. *Early Child Development and Care* 151: 11–17.

12. Field, T. M. (1999). American adolescents touch each other less and are more aggressive toward their peers as compared with French adolescents. *Adolescence* 34: 753–758.

13. Older, J. (1982). *Touching Is Healing*. New York: Stein and Day, 86.

14. Ibid., 129.

15. Ibid., 196.

16. Montagu, *Touching,* 270.

17. Older, *Touching Is healing*, 179.

18. Ibid., 165.

19. Ibid., 181.

20. Field, T. M. (1998). Massage therapy effects. *American Psychologist* 53: 1270–1281.

Chapter 2

1. Montagu, *Touching*, 340.

2. Ibid., 341.

3. Field, T. M. (1999). American adolescents touch each other less and are more aggressive toward their peers as compared with French adolescents. *Adolescence* 34: 753–758.

4. Douglas, J. (1978). Pioneering a non-western psychology. *Science News* 113: 154–158.

5. Prescott, J. W., and Wallace, D. (1976). Developmental Sociobiology and the origins of aggressive behavior. Paper presented at the 21st International Congress of Psychology, July 18–25, Paris.

6. Mead, M. (1935). *Sex and Temperament in Three Primitive Societies*. New York: William Morrow, 40–41.

7. Konner, M. J. (1976). Maternal care, infant behavior and development among the !Kung. In R. B. Lee and I. DeVore (eds.), *Kalahari Hunter-Gatherers*. Cambridge, Mass.: Harvard University Press, 219–245.

8. Montagu, *Touching*, 358.

9. Ibid., 359.

10. Radcliffe-Brown, A. R. (1933). *The Andaman Islanders*. Cambridge: Cambridge University Press, 117.

11. Cohen, S. (1987). *The Magic of Touch*. New York: Harper & Row, 146.

12. Jourard, S. M. (1966). An exploratory study of body accessibility. *British Journal of Social and Clinical Psychology* 5: 221–231.

13. Montagu, A. (1995). Animadversions on the development of a theory of touch. In Field et al., *Touch in Early Development*, 1–10.

14. Older, *Touching Is Healing*, 161.

15. Heslin, R., and Patterson, M. L. (1982). *Nonverbal Behavior and Social Psychology*. New York: Plenum.

16. Crusco, A., and Wetzel, C. G. (1973). Touch. *Journal of Personality and Social Psychology* 10: 21–29.

17. Fisher, J., Rytting, M., and Heslin, R. (1976). Affective and evaluative effects of an interpersonal touch. *Sociometry* 39: 416–421.

18. Fisher, J. A., and Gallant, S. J. (1990). Effect of touch on hospitalized patients. In Gunzenhauser, N., Brazelton, T. B., and Field,

T. M. (eds.), *Advances in Touch*. Skillman, N.J.: Johnson & Johnson, 141–147.

19. Henley, N. (1977). *Body Politics: Power, Sex and Nonverbal Communication*. Englewood Cliffs, N.J.: Prentice-Hall.

20. Major, B. (1990). Gender and status patterns in social touch. The impact of setting and age. In Gunzenhauser, Brazelton, and Field, *Advances in Touch*, 148–154.

21. Cigales, M., Field, T. M., Hossain, Z., Pelaez-Nogueras, M., and Gewirtz, J. (1996). Touch among children at nursery school. *Early Child Development and Care* 126: 101–110.

22. Triplett, J., and Arneson, S. (1979). The use of verbal and tactile comfort to alleviate distress in young hospitalized children. *Research in Nursing and Health* 2: 22.

23. Montagu, *Touching*, 393.

24. Cohen, *The Magic of Touch*, 49.

25. Kennedy, A. P., and Dean, S. (1986). *Touching for Pleasure*. Chatsworth, Calif.: Chatsworth Press.

26. O'Neil, P. M., and Calhoun, K. S. (1975). Sensory deficits and behavioral deterioration in senescence. *Journal of Abnormal Psychology* 84: 579–582.

27. Luce, G. (1979). *Your Second Life*. New York: Basic Books.

28. Lynch, J. (1977). *The Broken Heart*. New York: Basic Books.

29. Field, T. M., Hernandez-Reif, M., Quintino, O., Schanberg, S., and Kuhn, C. (1998). Elder retired volunteers benefit from giving massage therapy to infants. *Journal of Applied Gerontology* 17: 229–239.

Chapter 3

1. Levine, S. (1962). Plasma-free corticosteroid response to electric shock in rats stimulated in infancy. *Science* 135: 795–796.

2. Dennenberg, V. (1990). In Gunzenhauser, Brazelton, and Field, *Advances in Touch*, 3–10.

3. Meaney, M. J., Aitken, D. H., Bhatnagar, S., Bodnoff, S. R., Mitchell, J. B., and Sarrieau, A. (1990). Neonatal handling and the development of the adrenocortical response to stress. In Gunzenhauser, Brazelton, and Field, *Advances in Touch*, 11–21.

4. Field, T. M. (1998). Massage therapy effects. *American Psychologist* 53: 1270–1281.

5. Modi, Neena, et al., MRI study in progress.

6. Harlow, H., and Zimmerman, R. R. (1958). The development of affectional responses in infant monkeys. *Proceedings, American Philosophical Society* 102: 501–509.

7. Suomi, S. J. (1995). Touch and the immune system in rhesus monkeys. In Field, T. M. (ed.), *Touch in Early Development*, 89–103.

8. Jean-Pierre LeCanuet, personal commuication.

9. Uvnas-Moberg, K. (1996). Neuroendocrinology of the mother-child interaction. *Trends in Endocrinology and Metabolism* 7: 126–131.

10. Field, T. M., Hernandez-Reif, M., Hart, S., Theakston, H., Schanberg, S., Kuhn, C., and Burman, I. (1999). Pregnant women benefit from massage therapy. *Journal of Psychosomatic Obstetrics and Gynecology* 20: 31–38.

11. Leboyer, F. (1975). *Birth Without Violence*. New York: Basic Books.

12. Klaus, M. (1995). Touching during and after childbirth. In Field, T. M. (ed.), *Touch in Early Development*, 19–33.

13. Kennell, J. (1990). Doula-mother and parent-infant contact. In Gunzenhauser, Brazelton, and Field, *Advances in Touch*, 53–61.

14. Klaus, M. (1995). Touching during and after childbirth. In Field, T. M. (ed.), *Touch in Early Development*, 19–31.

15. Field, T. M., Hernandez-Reif, M., Taylor, S., Quintino, O., and Burman, I. (1997). Labor pain is reduced by massage therapy. *Journal of Psychosomatic Obstetrics and Gynecology* 18: 286–291.

16. Field, T. M., Grizzle, N., Scafidi, F., and Schanberg, S. (1996). Massage and relaxation therapies' effects on depressed adolescent mothers. *Adolescence* 31: 903–911.

17. Jones, N. A., and Field, T. M. (1999). Massage and music therapies attentuate frontal EEG asymmetry in depressed adolescents. *Adolescence* 34: 529–534.

18. Kennell, J., Doula mother, 57.

19. Klaus, M., and Kennell, J. (1982). *Parent-Infant Bonding*, 2d ed., St. Louis: Mosby.

20. Kennell, J., Doula mother, 59.

21. Kaitz, M., Lapidot, P., Bronner, R., and Eidelman, A. I. (1992). Parturient women can recognize their infants by touch. *Developmental Psychology* 28: 35–39.

22. Kaitz, M., Shiri, S., Danziger, S., Hershko, Z., and Eidelman, A. I. (1994). Fathers can also recognize their newborns by touch. *Infant Behavior and Development* 17: 205–207.

23. Kaitz, M. (1992). Recognition of familiar individuals by touch. *Physiology and Behavior* 52: 565–567.

24. Shirley, M. (1939). A behavior syndrome characterizing prematurely-born children. *Child Development* 10: 115–128.

25. Field, T. M., Sandberg, D., Quetel, T. A., Garcia, R., and Rosario, M. (1985). Effects of ultrasound feedback on pregnancy anxiety, fetal activity and neonatal outcome. *Obstetrics and Gynecology* 66: 525–528.

26. Abrams, S. M., Field, T. M., Scafidi, F., and Prodromidis, M. (1995). Newborns of depressed mothers. *Infant Mental Health Journal* 16: 231–237.

27. Lundy, B., Field, T. M., Cigales, M., Cuadra, A., and Pickens, J. (1997). Vocal and facial expression matching in infants of mothers with depressive symptoms. *Infant Mental Health Journal* 18: 265–273.

28. Hernandez-Reif, M. (2000). Perception of newborns. Paper presented at International Conference on Infant Studies, Brighton, England.

29. Jones, N. A., Field, T., Fox, N. A., Davalos, M., Lundy, B., and Hart, S. (1998). Newborns of mothers with depressive symptoms are physiologically less developed. *Infant Behavior and Development* 21: 537–541.

30. Lundy, B. L., Jones, N. A., Field, T., Nearing, G., Davalos, M., Pietro, P., Schanberg, S., and Kuhn, C. (1999). Prenatal depression effects on neonates. *Infant Behavior and Development* 22: 121–137.

31. Lundy, B. L., Field, T., Cuadra, A., Nearing, G., Cigales, M., and Hashimoto, M. (1996). Mothers with depressive symptoms touching newborns. *Early Development and Parenting* 5: 129–134.

32. Dieter, J., Field, T. M., Jones, N. A., Lecanuet, J. P., Hernandez-Reif, M., and Salman, F. A. (2001). Maternal depression and increased fetal activity, *Obstetrics and Gynecology*, in press.

33. Hofer, M. A. (1975). Infant separation responses and the maternal role. *Biological Psychiatry* 10: 149–153.

34. Gottfried, A. W. (1984). Environment of newborn infants in special care units. In Gottfried, A. W., and Gaiter, J. L. (eds.), *Infants Stress Under Intensive Care:* Environmental Neonatology. Baltimore: University Park Press, 28–41.

35. Field, T. M., and Goldson, E. (1984). Pacifying effects of nonnutritive sucking on term and preterm neonates during heelstick procedures. *Pediatrics* 74: 1012–1015.

36. Field, T. M., Schanberg, S. M., Scafidi, F., Bauer, C. R., Vega-Lahr, N., Garcia, R., Nystrom, J., and Kuhn, C. M. (1986). Tactile/kinesthetic stimulation effects on preterm neonates. *Pediatrics* 77: 654–658.

37. Neal, M. (1968). Vestibular stimulation and developmental behavior of the small, premature infant. *Nursing Research Reports* 3: 2–5.

38. Freedman, D., Boverman, H., and Freedman, N. (1966). Effects of kinesthetic stimulation on weight gain and on smiling in premature infants. Paper presented at the American Orthopsychiatric Association, San Francisco.

39. Rausch, P. B. (1981). Effects of tactile and kinesthetic stimulation on premature infants. *Journal of Obstetrics, Gynecology and Neonatal Nursing* 10: 34.

40. White, J., and LaBarba, R. (1976). The effects of tactile and kinesthetic stimulation on neonatal development in the premature infant. *Developmental Psychobiology* 9: 569–577.

41. Korner, A. F., Ruppel, E. M., and Rho, J. M. (1982). Effects of water beds on the sleep and mobility of theophylline-treated preterm infants. *Pediatrics* 70: 864–869.

42. Thoman, E. B., and Ingersoll, E. W. (1988). Prematures do like the breathing bear. Poster presented at the International Conference on Infant Studies, Washington, D.C.

43. Salk, L. (1960). The effects of the normal heartbeat sound on the behavior of the newborn infant: Implications for mental health. *World Mental Health* 12: 1–8.

44. Field, T. M., Ignatoff, E., Stringer, S., Brennan, J., Greenberg, R., Widmayer, S., and Anderson, G. (1982). Nonnutritive sucking during tube feedings: Effects on preterm neonates in an ICU. *Pediatrics* 70 (3): 381–384.

45. Field, T. M., Woodson, R., Greenberg, R., and Cohen, D. (1982) Discrimination and imitation of facial expressions by neonates. *Science* 218: 179–181.

46. Anderson, G. C. (1995). Touch and the kangaroo care method. In Field, T. M. (ed.), *Touch in Early Development*, 35–51.

47. Barr, R. (1990). Reduction of infant crying by parent carrying. In Gunzenhauser, Brazelton, and Field, *Advances in Touch*, 105–116.

48. Tronick, E. Z. (1995). Touch in mother-infant interaction. In Field, T. M. (ed.), *Touch in Early Development*, 53–65.

49. Montagu, A. (1995). Animadversions on the development of a theory of touch, 1–10.

50. Montagu, *Touching*, 204.

51. Morris, D. (1973). *Intimate Behavior*. New York: Bantam.

52. Landers, A. (1985). Sex: Why women feel short-changed. *Family Circle*, June 1985, 131–132.

53. Masters, W., and Johnson, V. (1970). *Human Sexual Inadequacy*, Boston: Little, Brown, 75.

54. Schanberg, S. (1995). The genetic basis for touch effects. In Field et al., *Touch in Early Development*, 67–79.

Chapter 4

1. Shipp, E. R. (1984). A puzzle for parents: Good touching or bad? *New York Times*, October 1984, C1, C12.

2. Montagu, A. (1995). Animadversions on the development of a theory of touch, 1–10.

3. Field, T. M., Harding, J., Soliday, B., Lasko, D., Gonzalez, N., and Valdeon, C. (1994). Touching in infant, toddler and preschool nurseries. *Early Child Development and Care* 98: 113–120.

4. Gergen, K. J., Gergen, M. M., and Barton, W. H. (1973). Deviance in the dark. *Psychology Today*, October, 129–130.

5. Field, T. M., Morrow, C., Valdeon, C., Larson, S., Kuhn, C., and Schanberg, S., (1992). Massage therapy reduces anxiety in child and adolescent psychiatric patients. *Journal of the American Academy of Child and Adolescent Psychiatry* 31: 125–131.

6. Howard, J. (1970). *Please Touch*. New York: Bantam.

7. Davis, G. (1971). *Touching*. Garden City Park, N.Y.: Avery Publishing Group.

8. Rogers, C. R. (1973). *Carl Rogers on Encounter Groups*. New York: Harper & Row, 146.

9. Gibb, J. R. (1970). The effects of human relations training. In Bergin, A. E. and Garfield, S. L. (eds.), *Handbook of Psychotherapy and Behavior Change*. New York: Wiley, 2114–2176.

10. Prescott, J. H. (1971). Early somatosensory deprivation as an ontogenetic process in the abnormal development of the brain and behavior. In Goldsmith, E. I. and Moor-Jankowski, J. (eds.), *Medical Primatology*. New York: S. Karger, 1–20.

11. Heinicke, C. M., and Westheimer, I. (1965). *Brief Separations*. New York: International Universities Press, 12.

12. Field, T. M., and Reite, M. (1984). Children's responses to separation from mother during the birth of another child. *Child Development 55*: 1308–1316; Field, T. M. (1991). Young children's adaptations to repeated separations from their mothers. *Child Development 62*: 539–547.

13. Suomi, S. J. (1995). Touch and the immune system in rhesus monkeys. In Field, T. M. (ed.), *Touch in Early Development*, 89–103.

14. Ironson, G., Field, T., Scafidi, F., Hashimoto, M., Kumar, M., Kumar, A., Price, A., Goncalves, A., Burman, I., Tetenman, C., Patarca, R., and Fletcher, M. A. (1996). Massage therapy is associated with enhancement of the immune system's cytotoxic capacity. *International Journal of Neuroscience 84*: 205–217.

15. Field, T. M., Grizzle, N., Scafidi, F., Abrams, S., and Richardson, S. (1996). Massage therapy for infants of depressed mothers. *Infant Behavior and Development 19*: 109–114.

16. Reite, M., and Capitanio, J. (1985). On the nature of social separation and social attachment. In Reite, M. and Field, T. M. (eds.), *The Psychobiology of Attachment and Separation*. Orlando, Fla.: Academic Press, 232–249.

17. Schanberg, S. (1995). The genetic basis for touch effects. In Field, T. M. (ed.), *Touch in Early Development*, 67–79.

18. Powell, G. F., Brasel, J. A., and Blizzard, R. M. (1967). Emotional deprivation and growth retardation stimulating ideopathic hypopituitarism. *New England Journal of Medicine 176*: 1271–1278.

19. Widdowson, E. M. (1951). Mental contentment and physical growth. *Lancet* 1: 1316–1318.

20. Montagu, Animadversions on the development of a theory of touch, 1–10.

21. Older, *Touching Is Healing*, 49.

22. Spitz, R. (1945). Hospitalism. *Psychoanalytic Study of the Child* 1: 53–74.

23. Dennis, W. (1973). *Children of the Creche*. New York: Penguin.

24. Dennis, W. (1977). Psychological response of patients with acute leukemia to germ-free environments. *Cancer, Journal of the American Cancer Society* 40: 871–879; Susman, E. J., Hollenbeck, A. R., Nannis, E. D., Strope, B. E., Hersh, S. P., Levine, A. S., and Pizzo, P. A. (1981). A prospective naturalistic study of the impact of an intensive medical treatment on the social behavior of child and adolescent cancer patients. *Journal of Applied Developmental Psychology* 2: 29–47.

25. Montagu, *Touching*, 266.

26. Older, *Touching Is Healing*, 79.

27. Waal, N. (1955). A special technique of psychotherapy with an autistic child. In Caplan, G. (ed.) *Emotional Problems of Early Childhood*. New York: Basic Books, 443–444.

28. Escalona, A., Field, T. M., Singer-Strunck, R., Cullen, C., and Hartshorn, K. (2001). Autism symptoms decrease following massage therapy, *Journal of Autism and Development*, in press.

29. Field, T. M., Lasko, D., Mundy, P., Henteleff, T., Talpins, S., and Dowling, M. (1997). Children with autism have improved attentiveness and responsivity after massage therapy. *Journal of Autism and Developmental Disorders* 27: 333–338.

30. Rosenthal, M. J. (1952). Psychosomatic study of infantile eczema. *Pediatrics* 10: 581–593.

31. Older, *Touching Is Healing*, 176.

32. Montagu, *Touching*, 282.

33. Field, T. M., Henteleff, T., Hernandez-Reif, M., Martinez, E., Mavunda, K., Kuhn, C., and Schanberg, S. (1998). Children with asthma have improved pulmonary functions after massage therapy. *Journal of Pediatrics* 132: 854–858.

34. Schachner, L., Field, T. M., Hernandez-Reif, M., Duarte, A. M., and Krasnegor, J. (1998). Atopic dermatitis symptoms decreased in

children following massage therapy. *Pediatric Dermatology* 15: 390–395.

35. Older, *Touching Is Healing*, 167.

36. Ibid.

37. Kraus, A. S., and Lillienfeld, A. M. (1959). Some epidemiological aspects of the high mortality rate in the young widowed group. *Journal of Chronic Diseases* 1: 207–217.

38. Carter, H., and Glick, P. C. (1970). *Massage and Divorce: A Social and Economic Study.* Cambridge: Harvard University Press.

39. Older, *Touching Is Healing*, 167.

40. Burke, J. (1993, Fall). Touch and wellness. *Touchpoints Newsletter* 1: 3.

Chapter 5

1. Montagu, A. (1995). Animadversions on the development of a theory of touch, 3, 20.

2. Montagu, *Touching*, 128, 366.

3. Montagu, Animadversions on the development of a theory of touch, 5.

4. Ibid., 7.

5. Cholewiak, R. W., and Collins, A. A., (1991). In Heller, M. A. and Schiff, W. (eds). *The Psychology of Touch*, Hillsdale, N.J.: Lawrence Erlbaum Associates, 24.

6. Ibid., 27.

7. Stephens, J. C. (1991). Thermal Sensitivity. In Heller and Schiff, *The Psychology of Touch*, 62.

8. Ibid., 63.

9. Sherrick, C. (1991). Vibrotactile pattern perception: Some findings and applications. In Heller and Schiff, *The Psychology of Touch*, 199.

10. Ibid., 199.

11. Oller, K. (1990). Tactile hearing for deaf children. In Gunzenhauser, Brazelton, and Field, *Advances in Touch*, 117.

12. Melzack, R. (1975). The McGill Pain Questionnaire: Major properties and scoring methods. *Pain* 1: 277–300.

13. Melzack, R., and Wall, P. D. (1988). *The Challenge of Pain.* London: Penguin.

14. Rollman, G. B. (1991). In Heller and Schiff, *The Psychology of Touch*, 101.

15. Field, T. M., Ironson, G., Pickens, J., Nawrocki, T., Fox, N., Scafidi, F., Burman, I., Schanberg, S., and Kuhn, C. (1996). Massage therapy reduces anxiety and enhances EEG pattern of alertness and math computations. *International Journal of Neuroscience* 86: 197–205.

Chapter 6

1. Eisenberg, D. M., Kessler, R. C., Foster, C., Norlock, F. E., Calkins, D. R., and Delbanco, T. L. (1993). Unconventional medicine in the United States: Prevalence, costs, and patterns of use. *New England Journal of Medicine*, January, 246–252.

2. Wolfson, L., Whipple, R., Derby, C., Judge, J., King, M., Amerman, P., Schmidt, J., and Smyers, D. (1996). Balance and strength training in older adults: Intervention gains and Tai Chi maintenance. *Journal of the American Geriatrics Society* 44: 498–506.

3. Kirsteins, A. E., Dietz, F., and Hwang, S. M. (1991). Evaluating the safety and potential use of a weight-bearing exercise, Tai-Chi Chuan, for rheumatoid arthritis patients. *American Journal of Physical Medicine and Rehabilitation* 70: 136–141.

4. Tse, S. K., and Bailey, D. M. (1998). Tai chi and postural control in the well elderly. *American Journal of Occupational Therapy* 46: 295–300.

5. Hartshorn, K., Delage, J., Field, T. M., and Olds, L. (2001). Senior citizens benefit from movement therapy. *Journal of Body Work and Movement Therapies* 5: 1–5.

6. Hernandez-Reif, M., Field, T. M., and Thimas, E. (2001). Attention deficit hyperactivity disorder benefit from Tai Chi. *Joural of Body Work and Movement Therapies* 5: 120–123.

7. Namikoshi, T. (1994). *Shiatsu: Japanese Finger Pressure Therapy.* New York: Japan Publications.

8. Eisenberg, D. (1985). *Encounters with Qi: Exploring Chinese Medicine.* New York: Norton and Co.

9. Older, *Touching Is Healing*, 87.

10. Ironson, G., Field, T., Scafidi, F., Hashimoto, M., Kumar, M., Kumar, A., Price, A., Goncalves, A., Burman, I., Tetenman, C., Patarca, R., and Fletcher, M. A. (1996). Massage therapy is associated with enhancement of the immune system's cytotoxic capacity. *International Journal of Neuroscience* 84: 205–217.

11. Inkeles, G. (1980). *The New Massage*. New York: Pedigree Books.

12. Downing, G. (1972). *The Massage Book*. New York: Bookworks.

13. Reich, W. (1949). *Character Analysis*. New York: Farrar, Straus, and Giroux; Reich, W. (1961). *The Function of the Orgasm*. New York: Farrar, Straus, and Giroux.

14. Cohen, S. (1987). *The Magic of Touch*. New York: Harper & Row, 105.

15. Ibid., 115.

16. Ackerman, D. (1990). *A Natural History of the Senses*. New York: Vintage, 119.

17. Older, *Touching Is Healing*, 251.

18. Anisfeld E., Casper, V., Nozyce, M., and Cunningham, N. (1990). Does infant carrying promote attachment? An experimental study of the effects of increased physical contact on the development of attachment. *Child Development* 61: 1617–1627.

19. Lozoff, B., and Buttenham, G. (1979). Infant Care: Cache or Cassy. *Journal of Pediatrics* 95: 478–483.

20. Field, T. M., and Goldson, E. (1984). Pacifying effects of nonnutritive sucking on term and preterm neonates during heelstick procedures. *Pediatrics* 74: 1012–1015.

21. Cohen, *The Magic of Touch*, 35.

Chapter 7

1. Mclure, V. S. (1989). *Infant Massage*. New York: Bantam.

2. Auckett, A. D. (1981). *Baby Massage*. New York: Newmarket Press.

3. Grossman, R. (1985). *The Other Medicines: An Invitation to Understanding and Using Them for Health and Healing*. Garden City, N.Y.: Doubleday and Co.

4. Eisenberg, *Encounters with Qi*.

5. Barnard, K. E., and Bee, H. L. (1983). The impact of temporally patterned stimulation on the development of preterm infants. *Child Development* 54: 1156–1167. Rausch, P. B. (1981). Neurophysiological development in premature infants following stimulation. *Developmental Psychology* 13: 69–76; Rice, R. D. (1977). Neurophysiological development in premature infants following stimulation. *Developmental Psychology* 13: 69–76; Solkoff, N., and Matuszak, D. (1975). Tactile stimulation and behavioral development among low-birthweight infants. *Child Psychiatry and Human Development* 6: 33–37; White, J. L., and LaBarba, R. C. (1976). The effects of tactile and kinesthetic stimulation on neonatal development in the premature infant. *Developmental Psychobiology* 6: 569–577.

6. Ottenbacher, K. J., Muller, L., Brandt, D., Heintzelman, A., Hojem, P., and Sharpe, P. (1987). The effectiveness of tactile stimulation as a form of early intervention: A quantitive evaluation. *Journal of Developmental and Behavioral Pediatrics* 8: 68–76.

7. Field, T. M., Schanberg, S., Scafidi, F., Bower, C., Vega-Lahr, N., Garcia, R., Nystrom, J., and Kuhn, C. M. (1986). Tactile/Kinesthetic Stimulation Effects on Preterm Neonates. *Pediatrics* 77: 654–658.

8. Jinon, S. (1996). The effect of infant massage on growth of the preterm infant. In Yarbes-Almirante, C., and De Luma, M. (eds.), *Increasing safe and successful pregnancy*. Netherlands: Elsevier Science, B.Z., 265–269.

9. Tang, C. (2001). Increased growth in preterm neonates following massage therapy. In review.

10. Goldstein-Ferber, S. (1997). Massage in premature infants. Paper presented at Child Development Conference, Bar-Elon, Israel.

11. White-Traut, R. C., and Nelson, M. N. (1988). Maternally administered tactile, auditory, visual, and vestibular stimulation: Relationship to later interactions between mothers and premature infants. *Research in Nursing and Health* 11: 31–39.

12. Acolet, D., Giannakoulopoulos, X., Bond, C., Weg, W., Clow, A., and Glover, V. (1993). Changes in plasma cortisol and catecholamine concentrations in response to massage in preterm infants. *Archives of Disease in Childhood* 68: 29–31.

13. Schanberg, S., and Field, T. M. (1988). Maternal deprivation and supplemental stimulation. In Field, T. M., McCabe, P., and Schneiderman, N. (eds.), *Stress and Coping across Development*. Hillsdale, N.J.: Lawrence Erlbaum Associates, 112–119.

14. Uvnas-Moberg, K., Widstrom, A. M., Marchine, G., and Windberg, J. (1987). Release of GI hormone in mothers and infants by sensory stimulation. *Acta Paediatrica Scandinavia* 76: 851–860.

15. Scafidi, F., Field, T. M., Wheeden, A., Schanberg, S., Kuhn, C., Symanski, R., Zimmerman, E., and Bandstra, E. S. (1996). Cocaine exposed preterm neonates show behavioral and hormonal differences. *Pediatrics* 97: 851–855.

16. Scafidi, F., and Field, T. M. (1997). Massage therapy improves behavior in neonates born to HIV positive mothers. *Journal of Pediatric Psychology* 21: 889–897.

17. Field, T., Hernandez-Reif, M., Hart, S., Theakston, H., Seharberg, S., Kuhn, C., and Burman, I. (1998). Pregnant women benefit from massage theraoy. *Journal of Psychosomatic Obstetrics and Gynecology* 20: 31–38.

18. Hansen, R., and Ulrey, G. (1988). Motorically impaired infants: Impact of a massage procedure on caregiver-infant interactions. *Journal of the Multihandicapped Person* 1: 61–68.

19. Field, T. M., Grizzle, N., Scafidi, F. Abrams, S., and Richardson, S. (1996). Massage therapy for infants of depressed mothers. *Infant Behavior and Development* 19: 109–114.

20. Scholz, K., and Samuels, C. A. (1992). Neonatal bathing and massage intervention with fathers, behavioural effects 12 weeks after birth of the first baby: The Sunraysia Australia Intervention Project. *International Journal of Behavioral Development* 15: 67–81.

21. Cullen, C., Field, T. M., Escalona, A., and Hartshorn, K. (2001). Father-infant interactions are enhanced by massage therapy. *Early Child Development and Care* 164: 41–47.

22. Field, T. M., Hernandez-Reif, M., Quintino, O., Schanberg, S., and Kuhn, C. (1998). Elder retired volunteers benefit from giving massage therapy to infants. *Journal of Applied Gerontology* 17: 229–239.

23. Campion, E., Berkman, B., and Fulmer, T. (1986). Failure to thrive in the elderly. Hospital Survey, unpublished report, Harvard Medical School.

24. Copeland, J. R. M., Dewey, M. E., Wood, N., Searle, R., Davidson, I. A., and McWilliams, C. (1987). Range of mental illness among the elderly in the community: Prevalence in Liverpool using the GMS-AGECAT package. *British Journal of Psychiatry* 150: 815–823.

25. Gaylord, S. A., and Zung, W. W. K. (1987). Affective disorders among the aging. In Carstensen, L. L. and Edelstein, B. A. (eds.), *Handbook of Clinical Gerontology*, New York: Pergamon Books, 214–219.

26. Post, F. (1982). Functional disorder II. Treatment and its relationship to causation. In Levy, R. and Post, F. (eds.), *The Psychiatry of Late Life*, London: Blackwell Scientific.

27. Grossberg, J. M., and Alf, E. F., Jr. (1985). Interaction with pet dogs: Effects on human cardiovascular response. *Journal of the Delta Society*, 20–27.

Chapter 8

1. Older, *Touching Is Healing*, 86.

2. Ibid., 90.

3. Ibid., 92.

4. Field, T. M., Ironson, G., Pickens, J., Nawrocki, T., Fox, N., Scafidi, F., Burman, I., Schanberg, S., and Kuhn, C. (1996). Massage therapy reduces anxiety and enhances EEG pattern of alertness and math computations. *International Journal of Neuroscience* 86: 197–205.

5. Field, T. M., Lasko, D., Mundy, P., Henteleff, T., Talpins, S., and Dowling, M. (1996). Autistic children's attentiveness and responsivity improved after touch therapy. *Journal of Autism and Developmental Disorders* 27 (3): 333–338.

6. Escalona, A., Field, T. M., Singer-Strunck, R., Cullen, C., and Hartshorn, K. (2001). Autism symptoms decrease following massage therapy. *Journal of Autism and Developmental Disability*, in press.

7. Field, T. M., Quintino, O., Hernandez-Reif, M., and Koslovsky, G. (1998). Adolescents with attention deficit hyperactivity disorder benefit from massage therapy. *Adolescence* 33: 103–108.

8. Field, T. M., et al. (1994). Massage for abused and neglected children. Unpublished data.

9. Field, T. M., Seligman, S., Scafidi, F., and Schanberg, S. (1996). Alleviating posttraumatic stress in children following Hurricane Andrew. *Journal of Applied Developmental Psychology* 17: 37–50.

10. Field, T. M., Morrow, C., Valdeon, C., Larson, S., Kuhn, C., and Schanberg, S. (1992). Massage therapy reduces anxiety in child and

adolescent psychiatric patients. *Journal of the American Academy of Child and Adolescent Psychiatry* 31: 125–131.

11. Field, T. M., Schanberg, S., Kuhn, C., Fierro, K., Henteleff, T., Mueller, C., Yando, R., Shaw, S., and Burman, I. (1998). Bulimic adolescents benefit from massage therapy. *Adolescence* 33: 555–563.

12. Field, T. M., Sunshine, W., Hernandez-Reif, M., Quintino, O., Schanberg, S., Kuhn, C., and Burman, I. (1997). Chronic fatigue syndrome: Massage therapy effects on depression and somatic symptoms in chronic fatigue syndrome. *Journal of Chronic Fatigue Syndrome* 3: 43–51.

13. Adcock, C. L. (1987). Massage therapy in alcohol/drug treatment. *Alcoholism Treatment Quarterly* 1: 87–101.

14. Hernandez-Reif, M., Field, T. M., and Hart, S. (1999). Smoking cravings are reduced by self-massage. *Preventive Medicine* 28: 28–32.

15. Field, T. M., Hernandez-Reif, M., Quintino, O., Schanberg, S., and Kuhn, C. (1998). Elder retired volunteers benefit from giving massage therapy to infants. *Journal of Applied Gerontology* 17: 229–239.

16. Jones, N. A., and Field, T. M. (1999). Right frontal EEG asymmetry is attenuated by massage and music therapy. *Adolescence* 34: 529–534.

17. Field, T. M., Hernandez-Reif, M., Taylor, S., Quintino, O., Burman, I., Kuhn C., and Schanberg, S. (1997). Labor pain is reduced by massage therapy. *Journal of Psychosomatic Obstetrics and Gynecology* 18: 286–291.

18. Field, T. M., Peck, M., Krugman, S., Tuchel, T., Schanberg, S., Kuhn, C., and Burman, I. (1998). Burn injuries benefit from massage therapy. *Journal of Burn Care and Rehabilitation* 19: 241–244.

19. Hernandez-Reif, M., Field, T. M., Largie, S., Hart, S., Redzepi, M., Nieremberg, B., and Peck, M. (2001). Children's distress during burn treatments is reduced by massage therapy. *Journal of Burn Care and Rehabilitation* 22.

20. Field, T. M., Peck, M., Hernandez-Reif, M., Krugman, S., Burman, I., and Ozment-Schenck, L. (2000). Postburn itching, pain and psychological symptoms are reduced by massage therapy. *Journal of Burn Care and Rehabilitation* 21: 189–193.

21. Lepresle, M. I., Mechet, C., and Debesse, B. (1991). Postoperative pain after thoracotomy. A study of 116 patients. *Revue Des Maladies Respiratoires* 8: 213–218.

22. Field, T. M., Hernandez-Reif, M., Seligman, S., Krasnegor, J., Sunshine, W., Rivas-Chacon, R., and Schanberg, S. (1997). Juvenile rheumatoid arthritis patients benefit from massage therapy. *Journal of Pediatric Psychology* 22: 607–617.

23. Melzack, R., and Wall, P. D. (1988). *The Challenge of Pain.* London: Penguin.

24. Hernandez-Reif, M., Field, T. M., Dieter, J., Swerdlow, B., and Diego, M. (1998). Migraine headaches are reduced by massage therapy. *International Journal of Neuroscience* 96: 1–11.

25. Sunshine, W., Field, T. M., Schanberg, S., Quintino, O., Kilmer, T., Fierro, K., Burman, I., Hashimoto, M., McBride, C., and Henteleff, T. (1996). Massage therapy and transcutaneous electrical stimulation effects on fibromyalgia. *Journal of Clinical Rheumatology* 2: 18–22.

26. Puustjarvi, K., Airaksinen, O., and Pontinen, P. J. (1990). The effects of massage in patients with chronic tension headache. *Acupuncture and Electro-Therapeutic Research* 15: 159–162.

27. Hernandez-Reif, M., Field, T., Krasnegor, J., Theakston, H., and Burman, I. (2000). Chronic lower back pain is reduced and range of motion increased after massage therapy. *International Journal of Neuroscience* 99: 1–15.

28. Weinrich, S. P., and Weinrich, M. C. (1990). The effect of massage on pain in cancer patients. *Applied Nursing Research* 3: 140–145.

29. Naliboff, B. D., and Tachiki, K. H. (1991). Autonomic and skeletal muscle responses to nonelectrical cutaneous stimulation. *Perceptual and Motor Skills* 72: 575–584.

30. Kaada, B., and Torsteinbo, O. (1989). Increase of plasma beta-endorphins in connective tissue. *General Pharmacology* 20: 487–490.

31. Melzack et al., op. cit.

32. Sunshine et al., op. cit.

33. Hernandez-Reif, M., Ironson, G., Field, T. M., Largie, S., Diego, M., Mora, D., and Bornstein, J. (2001). Children with Down syndrome improved in motor function and muscle tone following massage therapy. *Journal of Early Interventions*, in press.

34. Hernandez-Reif, M., Field, T. M., Largie, S., Diego, M., Manigat, N., Seonanes, J., Bornstein, J., and Waldman, R. (2001). Cerebral Palsy symptoms in children decreased following massage therapy. *Journal of Early Intervention*, in review.

35. Hernandez-Reif, M., Field, T. M., and Theakston, H. (1998). Multiple Sclerosis patients benefit from massage therapy. *Journal of Bodywork and Movement Therapies* 2: 168–174.

36. Diego, M., Hernandez-Reif, M., Field, T. M., Brucker, B., Hart, S., and Burman, I. (2001). Spinal cord injury benefits from massage therapy. *Journal of Bodywork and Movement Therapies*, in press.

37. Field, T. M., Henteleff, T., Hernandez-Reif, M., Martinez, E., Mavunda, K., Kuhn, C., and Schanberg, S. (1998). Children with asthma have improved pulmonary functions after massage therapy. *Journal of Pediatrics* 132: 854–858.

38. Field, T. M., Shaw, K. H., and LaGreca, A. (1996). Massage therapy lowers blood glucose levels in children with diabetes mellitus. *Diabetes Spectrum* 10: 237–239.

39. Schachner, L., Field, T. M, Hernandez-Reif, M., Duarte, A., and Krasnegor, J. (1998). Atopic dermatitis symptoms decrease in children following massage therapy. *Pediatric Dermatology* 15: 390–395.

40. Green, R. G., and Green, M. L. (1987). Relaxation increases salivary immunoglobulin A. *Pychological Reports* 61: 623–629.

41. Sims, S. (1986). Slow stroke back massage for cancer patients. *Nursing Times* 82: 47–50.

42. Hernandez-Reif, M., Field, T. M., Ironson, G., Weiss, S., and Katz, G. (2001). Breast cancer patients have improved immune functions following massage therapy, in review.

43. Field, D. A., and Miller S. (1992). Cosmetic breast surgery. *American Family Physician* 45: 711–719.

44. Ironson, G., Field, T. M., Scafidi, F., Kumar, M., Patarca, R., Price A., Gonclaves, A., Hashimoto, M., Kumar, A., Burman, I., Tetenman, C., and Fletcher, M. A. (1996). Massage therapy is associated with enhancement of the immune system's cytotoxic capacity. *International Journal of Neuroscience* 84: 205, 218.

45. Diego, M., Hernandez-Reif, M., Field, T. M., Friedman, L., and Shaw, K. (2001). Massage therapy effects on immune function in adolescents with HIV. *International Journal of Neuroscience* 106: 35–45.

Index

during painful events and
procedures, 140–143 (*see
also* Labor)
theories about why massage
produces, 146–147
therapies for, 85–86 (*see also
specific therapies*)
Pets, 10, 30
Pet therapy, 30–31
Pheromones, 53
Play, 110–111
Polarity therapy, 101–102
Postoperative pain, 142–143
Postpartum depression, 42–43
Posttraumatic stress disorder
(PTSD), 136–137
Pregnancy, touch during, 36–37
Pregnant women, massaging
to prevent premature births,
124
Premature infants, vii
infant massage with, 119–124
Preschool, 2, 27, 60
Psychiatric inpatients, 61, 137
Public behavior, effects of touch
on, 24
Public displays of affection, 10,
12–13

Rats, viii, 33–34, 44, 47, 67,
123
Reflexology, 95–97
Rheumatoid arthritis, juvenile,
143–144
Rough and tumble play, 110

SAGE, 30
Schanberg, Saul, viii, 57, 67–68
Schools, 2, 111. *See also*
Preschool

fear of sexual abuse and
prohibitions against touch,
2–5, 59–60
Self-touch, 13, 113–115. *See
also* Massaging oneself
Sensate Focus System, 56, 112–113
Sensory aids, 82–83
Separation, early, 40, 43–45
Sex, touch between persons of
opposite *vs.* same, 24, 26,
62
Sex differences, 25–27, 56
in frequency of being touched,
9, 25–27
in reactions to touch, 9–10,
24–25, 56
Sex touch therapies, 56, 112–113
Sexual abuse. *See* Child
(sexual) abuse
Sexual harassment laws, 4–5
Sexual intercourse, 53
Sexually promiscuous behavior
fear of, 61
in response to touch-
deprivation, 53
Sexual stimulation, fear of, 7
Sexual taboos, 14
Sexual *vs.* nonsexual, touch
interpreted as, 26
Shiatsu, 92, 93
Skin, 76, 78
functions, 76–79
Skincare, touch, 108–109
Skin problems, 72
Sleep deficits, 146–147
Sleep problems, 63–65
massage with infants who
have, 118–119
Smoking cessation, 139